BUILDING BIGGER IDEAS

BUILDING BIGGER IDEAS

A Process for Teaching Purposeful Talk

Maria Nichols

HEINEMANN
PORTSMOUTH, NH

Heinemann
361 Hanover Street
Portsmouth, NH 03801–3912
www.heinemann.com

Offices and agents throughout the world

The author and publisher wish to thank those who have generously given permission to reprint borrowed material:

Figure 1.1: From *This Is a Book* by Demetri Martin, copyright © 2011, 2012. Reprinted by permission of Grand Central Publishing, a subsidiary of Hachette Book Group, Inc.

Figure 1.2: Adapted from *This Is a Book* by Demetri Martin, copyright © 2011, 2012. Reprinted by permission of Grand Central Publishing, a subsidiary of Hachette Book Group, Inc.

Cataloging-in-Publication data is on file at the Library of Congress.
ISBN: 978-0-325-09815-9

Editor: Katie Wood Ray
Production: Victoria Merecki
Cover and text designs: Monica Ann Crigler
Front cover photo: Tyler Hulett/Getty Images
Typesetter: Shawn Girsberger
Manufacturing: Steve Bernier

Printed in the United States of America on acid-free paper
23 22 21 20 19 RWP 1 2 3 4 5

To the educators
and children
who've welcomed me
into their communities
and their conversations.
Thank you for
your openness, trust, and
an endless abundance
of joy.

Contents

Acknowledgments

*In life, as in jazz,
there is great beauty in collaboration.*

~ Herbie Hancock

I'm in the airport, making the best of flight delays by meandering through the bookstore, when I stumble upon Herbie Hancock's *Possibilities* (2015). An autobiography about a musician? Not my usual, but something about the cover photo draws me in. I pick up a copy, begin to thumb through, and find myself completely hooked on page one.

What captivates me so quickly are Hancock's reminiscings about a gig with the Miles Davis Quintet early on in his career. That night, as Hancock describes it, the band was "tight." There was a magical feeling in the air as they built toward one of Davis' infamous solos, and everything was going so right—until Hancock played a chord that was so wrong.

That chord, Hancock recalls, was ". . . hanging out there like a piece of rotten fruit." But, then, the unexpected happened. Without missing a beat, Davis picked up that chord—the one Hancock felt was so wrong—and lifted it into pure magic. Hancock reflects, ". . . Miles never judged it—he just heard it as a sound that happened, and he instantly took it on as a challenge . . . And because he didn't judge it, he was able to run with it, to turn it into something amazing" (2015, 2).

These lines fueled my entire flight home. I realize now that Davis' reaction—his willingness to suspend judgment and run with the unexpected—has everything to do with dialogic processing. In the dialogic

ix

classroom, the unexpected is routine. That's part of the thrill. Being open, willing, and confident to take in unexpected thoughts, withhold judgment, and run with them is, in big part, what this book is about.

As compelling as that is, Davis' stance also speaks to me on another level. In that moment, Davis embodied everything I value in the colleagues I'm privileged to learn with and from day in and day out. Open-minded, curious, and passionate educators who embrace the new and the unexpected—not with choruses of "No!" or "That's not how . . . !" but with "Hmmm" and "What if . . ." and "Let's try . . ." Willing to riff off of unexpected ideas the ways Miles Davis took off with Hancock's chord, working them into possibilities.

My thank-yous to these people have to begin with Katie Wood Ray, who approached our work together with a gentle heart, a keen eye, and a laser-like focus on practicality. She listened, questioned, and nudged for reflection, and in doing so, helped to organize and lift a wild range of thinking. Because of Katie, Patty Adams, Victoria Merecki, and Monica Crigler, this book is more than I thought possible.

As always, I'm appreciative of my longtime friend, colleague, and thought partner Debra Crouch. Debra's my first go-to when I know I'm risking a "wrong chord." She's always willing to dive in and find possibility in the wildest of notions.

I'm incredibly fortunate to have feedback into my thoughts and practices from Peter Johnston. To be alongside Peter in a classroom is to see the previously invisible, question the previously accepted, and wonder anew. His encouragement, questions, and suggestions always open new possibilities, and push me a step or two beyond where I thought I was heading.

This book would not be possible without the classroom teachers and children, many of whom you'll meet in the pages to come, who were willing to welcome me into their communities to think and talk alongside them. I'm in awe of the possibilities they create together.

I'm endlessly thankful for longtime friends and colleagues like Susie Althof, Cherissa Beck, Pat and Bill Eastman, Kathy Champeau, Sarah Trueblood, and Jeralyn Johnson. Thinking, talking, and simply being with these people energize me. An extra big thank-you goes to Rob Corona, who listened with intent as I described what I thought purposeful talk looked like, questioned in ways that nudged me to clarify, and then created the vibrant, dynamic images of purposeful talk for this text.

Big thank-yous also go to my family: my mother, whose memory continues to inspire; my father, who, at ninety-three, still strives to learn every day; my brother, sister-in-law, and nieces, who bring joy; and my sister Cris, who cheers me on and sends ridiculously cute and hopelessly distracting pictures of her dogs at all the right times.

And most importantly, to Rick, whose patience with my passion for this work admittedly stretches, but never breaks—thank you!

Introduction

Beginning with the End

I was hovering over the dining room table alongside my friend and colleague Debra Crouch—computers, texts, journals, and sticky notes scattered about. We had challenged ourselves into a conversation about what it means to be a teacher of thinkers, and were in that rapid ideation phase of the work, with tentative ideas ranging far and wide.

As we wrestled though the possibilities, no matter what the angle on teaching thinkers, the role of purposeful talk naturally emerged. Debra finally plopped down a well-worn copy of my previous book, *Comprehension Through Conversation* (2006), and, by force of repeated use, it fell open to the last pages. With a laugh, Debra mused, "You know, it seems like I always begin conversations about this book with the end."

The "end" that Debra was referring to is an exploration of a reading conference with Jailyn—one of my third graders years ago. It was reading workshop, and I had been watching from across the room as Jailyn flipped the pages of Bruce McMillan's *Nights of the Pufflings* back and forth, seemingly mesmerized and puzzled, both at the same time. McMillan's narrative introduces readers to the children of a small Icelandic village, who come together each year to help newly hatched pufflings navigate human impediments to find their way to the sea. Curious, I naturally headed over to investigate. I sat down beside Jailyn and opened with my usual "What are you thinking?" Here's our conversation as recounted in the book:

> "I thought they [the children in the text] just do it to care for nature, but I know some kids [in our class] would say the people have to help," Jailyn explained, "because they shouldn't have lights and dogs where the pufflings have

to fly. So now I think they are caring, but maybe they also feel guilty 'cuz it's their lights that, like, well, that made the pufflings got lost."

"How do you know that some of the kids would think that?" I asked.

"Well, it's like when we talked about *The Great Kapok Tree*," Jailyn said, pointing in the general direction of the Rain Forrest tub in the nonfiction section of the library. "Some kids said the man shouldn't cut down the tree and live where the animals have to be. But people, they have to live places. But still, we thought they feel, like, well, guilty."

"Wow, what made you think of all of this?"

"When I'm reading, and, well, always I wonder, what would everybody— all the kids—how do they think about this?" (2006, 102–103)

Debra, I realized, had a point. I've been privileged to think alongside teachers, coaches, administrators, and district leaders across the United States and beyond about developing classrooms that are alive with purposeful talk. Inevitably, in the process of these conversations, Jailyn seems to wiggle her way in. I'll hear variations of, "You know, we want to create a school full of Jailyns." Or, "We want our students to be able to *use* talk to think and build new ideas, like Jailyn."

So, what is it about Jailyn's process that compels? To begin, she's the embodiment of Vygotsky's assertion that, "By giving our students practice in talking with others, we give them frames for thinking on their own" (1978, 19). But, I believe there's more to the aspiration than Jailyn's independent ability.

As educators, we all recognize that Jailyn's thinking developed in a classroom where she was supported by specific beliefs about teaching and learning, and about children's infinite capacity to soar when given the foundation, space, and support. In this environment, Jailyn learned that purposeful talk is a tool for constructing understanding with others. She came to value the diverse perspectives that would broaden and deepen her understanding, and she engaged in an inner-dialogue with these perspectives, developing empathy as she learned to see ideas and issues through the eyes of others.

No wonder Jailyn has inspired a small flotilla of professional journeys. But, teaching into this vision of possibility can be daunting. Figuring out exactly what we're aiming for and why, and where to start and how, may leave us teetering on the edge of our first steps, knowing we want to leap in, but not yet completely willing to let go.

Building Bigger Ideas is intended to pick up where *Comprehension Through Conversation* left off, addressing many of the questions I've explored with teachers, literacy coaches, and school and district leaders as they've worked to develop classrooms and schools that are alive with purposeful talk. Questions such as:

★   Why does teaching children to think and talk together purposefully matter?

★   How do we define this talk and use that definition to guide our efforts?

★   How do we teach into something as dynamic as purposeful talk and trust in children's ability to engage authentically?

★   How do we move children toward independence with purposeful talk?

Chapter One focuses on the *why* of purposeful talk, ensuring our efforts are consistently guided by a deep understanding. The chapter opens with a peek at talk in the classroom. Then, it moves beyond the classroom to explore purposeful talk "in the wild," drawing from collaborative endeavors and innovative environments that thrive on this talk. This exploration will help us define purposeful talk and develop a vision for what becomes possible when children engage daily with teaching and learning shaped by that vision.

For learning to "float on a sea of talk," as James Britton suggests (1983), children need the support of a brave learning community. These communities are places where children engage openly and honestly with each other, and with compelling, relevant—and often edgy—ideas. Chapter Two explores the ways teachers and children can develop the care, empathy, values, and understandings necessary for brave learning communities to thrive.

Then, Chapters Three through Six tackle the how of teaching purposeful talk, offering a process as dynamic as talk itself to engage children authentically and honestly. Chapter Three begins with Rupert

Wegerif's definition of dialogic classrooms as places where children learn *about* talk and *through* talk simultaneously, then briefly revisits three categories of talk behavior, first introduced in *Comprehension Through Conversation*, that support this learning. A process-oriented approach that engages children in **focus, facilitate,** and **feedback** cycles is the foundation for this teaching.

Chapters Four, Five, and Six offer a deeper dive into a range of talk moves that comprise each category of talk behavior. I'll explain how each talk move supports children's efforts to construct meaning, the challenges of teaching the moves, and ways we might focus, facilitate, and offer feedback for each. And lastly, Chapter Seven offers questions that help us to take an inquiry stance as we assess children's developing ability to use talk purposefully.

As you read, you'll find children's voices scattered throughout. These delightful voices, captured as the children thought and talked together, come from my own classroom, and from classrooms filled with teachers and children who've welcomed me in to learn alongside them. What I hope emerges from the children's talk is their brilliance, the depth of thinking and understanding that becomes possible when they engage through purposeful talk, and the sheer joy of dialogic classrooms.

If learning,

particularly that which

takes place in a classroom,

floats on a sea of talk,

what kind of talk?

And, what kind of

learning?

—Simpson and Mercer

One

Purposeful Talk in the World Beyond School

A Snapshot of Purposeful Talk

It's late spring, the end of the school year fast approaching, and I've timed a visit to an energetic fourth-grade classroom knowing I'll catch children immersed in reading workshop. My hope is to quietly observe for a bit, but Dominic spies me from across the room and makes a beeline in my direction. He skids into the seat next to me NASCAR pit-stop-style, plops a book on the table, and, looking at me with nothing but honest intent, asserts, "Mrs. Nichols, you're old, right?"

Torn between indignant denial and the earnestness of his inquiry, I hold my expression and manage a simple, "Why?"

Dominic urgently leans in. "No—we need more—see, we're trying to get—here, no—here!" Turning pages as fast as he's talking, Dominic lands on an illustration of soldiers hunkered in trenches. Nodding to Luis and Ana, who've now crowded around, Dominic continues, "We think it's all messed up."

"Yeah—really bad!" continues Luis, who tugs the book over to flip pages. "They have war [slapping an illustration of battle action for emphasis]. And then they have peace [now slapping an illustration of opposing soldiers playing soccer]. It's—they see how they can be the same—soccer, they give presents, singing . . ."

"And then," Dominic steps back in, flipping back to the soldiers in the trenches, "they go back in the holes—to be safe from bullets and stuff. They play soccer and then—why . . . ? It's—*whaaaat!*" [shaking his head and flinging his arms in the air with disbelief and more than a touch of drama].

"Yeah," Luis says, "We gotta get more thinking. 'Cuz we—all of us— think it's messed up!"

Uncertain, I pull the book over for a closer look. Immediately, I'm drawn into John McCutcheon's *Christmas in the Trenches*, a beautifully illustrated World War I narrative focused on the Christmas Truce of 1914. A grandfather's reminiscing and simple, muted illustrations reveal an inexplicable range of human complexity as warring sides lay down arms, raise the white flag, unite in the spirit of the holiday, and then retreat to their perspective trenches, ready to fight again the next day.

Clearly, the text has left Dominic, Luis, and Ana struggling with something far more complex than the facts of the truce itself. The group is wrestling with the logic of the Allied and German troops, trying to imagine themselves into the soldiers' minds to understand behavior that we, as adults, struggle to grasp.

> *Dominic, Luis, and Ana's ability with talk developed because their learning floated on a sea of talk— purposeful talk.*

As compelling as this intellectual struggle is, the trio's dialogic approach to the struggle is what really catches my attention. They're stuck, and are using their growing ability with talk to find a path forward. This didn't happen by chance. Dominic, Luis, and Ana's ability with talk developed because their learning floated on a sea of talk—*purposeful* talk.

Purposeful Talk in the World Beyond School

In this chapter, we'll explore what we mean by purposeful talk by taking a peak at groups that use talk productively "in the wild," in various arenas beyond school. This will help us better understand the generative potential of the talk Dominic, Luis, and Ana were using to explore the complex ideas suggested by a powerful text. But first, let's think about how we typically use talk in our everyday lives.

Imagine you're planning an evening out for dinner with a group of friends. Naturally, each of you has different thoughts on where to dine—Italian, Mexican, that new place midtown. One friend insists it's the best ever; another is quoting mediocre Yelp reviews. You barter, attempt to persuade, bird walk, joke, persuade some more, and finally coalesce when a Groupon coupon enters the conversation.

Yes, this is talk. It's talk that entertains, supports decision-making, and strengthens social bonds. In all those ways, it engages us for a reason. But this talk draws from what David Perkins refers to as "recipe knowledge" (2014, 59). We're talking to support doing something familiar, something we already know how to do. In fact, we know how to do it so well that we can minimally focus, allow our talk to meander, and in the end still succeed.

> **What happens when we're confronted with novel or challenging scenarios? When we need to problem-solve, innovate, or construct new understandings? How do we use talk then? What kind of talk? And, to what end?**

But what happens when we're confronted with novel or challenging scenarios? When we need to problem-solve, innovate, or construct new understandings? How do we use talk then? What kind of talk? And, to what end? Let's explore a small sampling of possibilities.

Talk in Competitive Team Sports

Adventure racing is an intense endurance competition. It combines navigation over an unmarked wilderness course with varying combinations of athletic disciplines including trekking, mountain biking, and paddling. It's not for the weekend warrior. Nor is it for lone competitors. Adventure racing is a team sport, requiring individuals who are not only physically up to the challenge, but who are able to collaborate, communicate, and problem-solve under very challenging circumstances.

In an extensive study of the dynamics of adventure-racing teams, Daniel Wilson, director of Harvard's Project Zero, analyzed their sense-making processes as they dealt with uncertainty during competition (2007). Wilson's analysis revealed key differences in the functioning of high-ranking and low-ranking teams, including their use of talk.

Wilson found that winning teams tended to take a collaborative approach to uncertainty, which he defined as moments of trying to figure

out where they were, how they were, and/or what to do next. To struggle
through this uncertainty, teams used talk for informational moves as they
gathered data; meaning making as they interpreted that data and theo-
rized; and action moves as they proposed and coordinated behaviors.

And, as they talked, Wilson found that winning teams tended toward
more conditional language—*we may be . . . , I think . . . , probably . . .*
—indicating a tentativeness that allowed for other perspectives, which
then enabled them to better share and interpret information and adapt
their strategy. Winning teams were also better at linking talk together,
working off the ideas of others to construct new understandings.

In short, successful teams stayed focused on intentional, mindful
means of interacting, purposefully using talk to draw from each voice and
construct productive theories and strategies. Wilson postulates that these
patterns of talk may be key to holding off premature decisions until the
wisdom of the collective reaches consensus.

Talk in the Innovation Economy

In "A Eulogy for the Private Office", author Cameron Herold writes
to report on the untimely death of—yes, the private office (2012). This
lighthearted send-off highlights a changing dynamic in successful business
cultures; a movement toward open environments designed for continuous
collaboration. What works in competitive team sports seems to be equally
valued in innovative business enterprises.

This shift is visible at Zappos, a retail leader that began its life as
the first online shoe store. CEO Tony Hsieh lauds a work environment
conducive to what he calls *serendipitous collisions*—unplanned interactions designed to increase collaboration, simply because that's how new
ideas happen. True to this vision, Zappos' Las Vegas headquarters boasts
a design engineered for serendipitous collisions. Included are a common
lobby that funnels people from every department into greater proximity
daily, elevators with video game screens intended to engage people in a
place where the norm is to disengage, and shared workspace, lounging
space, and eating space—all designed with talk in mind.

A belief in a culture of talk drives efforts at IDEO as well. Consistently
positioned atop lists of the world's most innovative companies, IDEO is
a global design firm that derives its success from a human-centered ap-

proach to problem-solving known as design thinking. In a 2013 *60 Minutes* interview, IDEO's co-founder, David Kelley, highlighted the collaborative nature of their design-thinking process by emphasizing the critical role of their design team's ability to talk together in very specific ways. With hands stair-stepping upward as he spoke for emphasis, Kelley explained:

> The big thing about *design thinking* is it allows people to build on the ideas of others . . . I come up with an idea, and then somebody from somewhere else says, "Oh that makes me think we should do this and then we could do that." And then you get to a place that you just can't get to in one mind.

Kelley's emphasis on the kind of talk that enables participants to build on the ideas of others is foundational to the structure of their design teams. These teams are deliberately constructed with a range of expertise, background, and perspective. The dialogic process Kelley describes allows teams to leverage this difference, and explore of a wide run of ideas during brainstorming. Their process provides time and space for thinking that emerges, diverges, and then gradually coalesces into an innovative whole—"a place that you just can't get to in one mind."

Talk in a Cutting-Edge Research Campus

The Salk Institute for Biological Studies was established by Jonas Salk with the goal of creating a collaborative physical and academic environment for biologic research. Jonas Salk's hope was to enable researchers to work together in ways that encouraged them "to consider the wider implications of their discoveries for the future of humanity" (Salk Institute for Biological Studies 2018).

The campus was designed by legendary architect Louis Kahn, whose buildings are described as having "a conviction about how you bring people together" (Miranda 2016). On a visit to the campus, I discovered that Jonas Salk added his touches to the physical design as well.

I set out for a scheduled tour of Salk with neurobiologist and outreach coordinator Ellen Potter. As I pulled off the main road, my navigation system announced I had "arrived," and halted guidance. Yet, as I attempted to find the designated parking lot and meeting place, I found myself going in circles. My problem-solving transitioned from looking in vain for signs and trying to reset the navigation, to pulling over to talk with no less than two security guards and a random scientist. As I shared my navigational woes with my tour partners, they all admitted to the same challenge. After a good laugh, Ellen connected our challenge to Jonas Salk's insistence on an environment designed for collaboration. It seems that Salk had signage on the campus kept to a minimum, necessitating conversation among people who might otherwise pass each other in silence. It worked!

Jonas Salk's emphasis on collaboration extends to the design and assignment of laboratory space as well. As Salk president William Brody explained:

> The beauty of Salk is that we don't have departments and structures, so we can have somebody working in viruses next to somebody in cancer next to somebody in neuroscience. And guess what? There may be a link between those three that leads to some major discovery. (Finkes 2014)

Essentially, the Salk Institute shunned a typical departmental organization with the intent of bringing difference together. As Thomas Albright, who oversees Salk's Center for the Neurobiology of Vision, observes, "My lab flows into the lab next to me, and that's the valuable thing . . . The sparks fly at the boundaries of different areas of scientific research" (Finkes 2014).

This belief in potential links between bodies of work, and the journey from link to major discovery, requires a particular dialogic stance. Like IDEO's design thinkers, Salk's scientists would need to talk together with the intent to "get to a place that you just can't get to in one mind."

Talk in the Affairs of Nations and Peoples

In his 1997 State of the Union address, President Bill Clinton spoke about the democratic foundation of the United States of America, stating:

> America is far more than a place. It is an idea, the most powerful idea in the history of nations. . . .We are now

the bearers of that idea, leading a great people into a new world.

With these words, Clinton highlights the dynamic nature of democracy, framing it as an evolving process that's at its strongest when we actively engage, and most apt to disappoint when we become complacent. An exploration of the kind of talk most likely to expand civic engagement points to a mix of constructive dialogue with intention to listen and understand, and deliberation involving critical thinking and reasoned argument (McCoy and Scully 2002).

This emphasis on listening was passionately embraced by Tennessee senator Howard Baker. When Baker passed away in June of 2014, he was widely honored as an eloquent listener, a trait Baker insisted was at the root of his success. White House Correspondent George E. Condon Jr. quoted Baker as saying, "I increasingly believe that the essence of leadership, the essence of good Senate service, is the ability to be an eloquent listener, to hear and understand what your colleagues have to say, what your party has to say, what the country has to say . . . and try to translate that into effective policy" (2014). Baker himself lamented that this "eloquent listening" was too often lacking in today's polarizing politics.

While an exploration of the degree to which Baker achieved the status of "eloquent listener" is beyond our purpose here, the notion is nonetheless captivating. Listening as an eloquent practice elevates it to an art form requiring a mindful, deliberate stance that recognizes the value of perspective in focused, constructive conversations.

This need to listen eloquently, and think and talk with others in productive ways, takes on added complexity when we consider that many of the issues we face today are a confluence of challenges—social, environmental, religious, economic, political, and beyond—that impact people in virtually every corner of the globe. Dr. Yong Zhao reminds us of the challenges of engaging and problem-solving globally:

> The globe has shrunk into an interconnected and interdependent village through global movements of goods, information, money, and people. But this village is new,

"Listening as an eloquent practice elevates it to an art form requiring a mindful, deliberate stance that recognizes the value of perspective in focused, constructive conversations."

its residents have just moved in, and they don't know one another very well. (2009, 1)

Engaging and problem-solving at a global level requires the ability to think and talk with people whose beliefs, experiences, and perspectives may be vastly different from our own. In *Solving Tough Problems: An Open Way of Talking, Listening, and Creating New Realities*, author Adam Kahane explores a dialogic approach to solving truly complex global issues—those that cross geographic, cultural, political, and economic boundaries. Kahane guides readers through a series of global scenarios requiring facilitated intervention. Each scenario reveals patterns of talk that span a dialogic continuum from closed talking and listening, which tends to use talk to *tell*, to more open forms of talking and listening, which use talk to *construct*. Using an example from socio-political strife in Argentina in 2001, Kahane outlines a successful dialogue as one that consists of multiple conversations over time, allowing ample opportunity for talk to diverge as a range of ideas are proposed, and then converge and deepen as participants construct new ideas together and plan forward (2007, 101).

It seems that, like the adventure-racing team members, the folks at IDEO, Zappos, and Salk, participants in high-stakes problem-solving do best when they think and talk together with the intent to construct ideas that are bigger, bolder, and more inclusive than they could possibly construct individually.

Defining Purposeful Talk

These descriptions of successful collaborations from the world beyond school reveal groups of people thinking and talking together in purposeful ways. They are not talking at each other, talking to rehearse or plan for the known, or talking to answer the kinds of questions that have right answers. Their talk has a purpose—and that purpose is to tackle the unknown—to strategize, to innovate, to problem-solve, to construct understanding. This use of talk "in the wild" frames the "why" behind purposeful talk in the classroom—our rationale for designing teaching and learning that's dialogic in nature.

In the explorations of talk in the scenarios above, three characteristics emerge. These three characteristics lead us to a definition of purposeful talk. Talk is purposeful when it

★ *honors constructive intent.* Purposeful talk engages participants in a deliberate process of building on a range of thinking to construct unique ideas, strategize, and innovate. Participants recognize their ability to draw from what Peter Senge describes as "a 'larger pool of meaning', accessible only to a group" (1990, 248), and believe deeply in the value of doing so.

★ *harnesses the power of varied perspectives.* Purposeful talk deliberately harnesses a range of perspectives to broaden and deepen the thinking and constructive potential. Participants value the differing perspectives, actively seek them out, and work to fully understand each voice.

★ *engages participants over expanded time and space.* Purposeful talk honors the time participants need to deepen and evolve understanding. Participants recognize that the process of constructing doesn't necessarily happen in simple, quick conversations. They're willing to dwell in shades of gray as they wrestle with varied perspectives, contemplate possibilities, and gather new thinking. They recognize that compelling ideas may linger and evolve over time, and are willing to cycle back to rethink and revise or expand previous understandings.

> *Their talk has a purpose—and that purpose is to tackle the unknown—to strategize, to innovate, to problem-solve, to construct understanding.*

Visualizing Purposeful Talk

Creating a visual image of a process as dynamic in nature as purposeful talk is challenging at best. But visuals are incredibly helpful for both internalizing the process, and pushing against misconceptions. So to give it a go, I'm going to stand on the shoulders of Demetri Martin. Martin (2012) tackled the challenge of representing success, an equally dynamic process, to highlight the disconnect between "what people think it looks like" and "what it really looks like" (Figure 1.1).

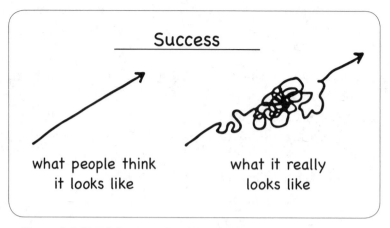

Figure 1.1 Martin's Representation of Success

This comparative image has been co-opted to represent misunderstandings of a range of dynamic processes, including learning (Figure 1.2).

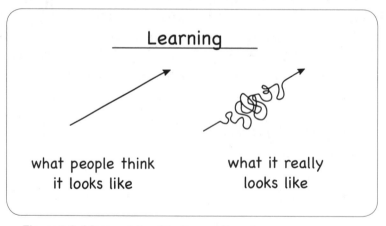

Figure 1.2 A Representation of the Process of Learning

In co-opting Martin's work to represent purposeful talk, I'm suggesting two images of "what people think it looks like," each touching on a very common misunderstanding. The first misunderstanding is that purposeful talk enables voices to quickly coalescence around a single answer or way of thinking, then move that thinking forward in a linear trajectory (Figure 1.3). In truth, when we're tackling novel and complex ideas, it takes both time and a circuitous path to build from tentative thoughts and wrestle with varied perspectives. While there may be times that agreement is achievable and necessary (such as with decisions in competitive racing or coalescence around a prototype), this isn't always the case.

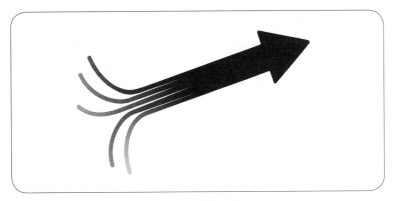

Figure 1.3 Voices Coalescing Around a Single Answer

Another misunderstanding of purposeful talk is equating it with a process more akin to voices talking in parallel (Figure 1.4). Participants may be talking about the same thing in the same space, but without any intent to construct. There is no eloquent listening, no grappling with perspectives, no effort to "get to a place that you just can't get to in one mind." Each participant tells their thinking, then leaves the shared space with that thinking unchanged.

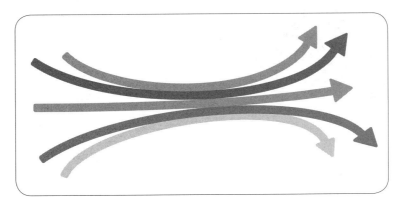

Figure 1.4 Voices Talking in Parallel

So what does purposeful talk really look like? Figure 1.5 captures the energy of voices *engaging with constructive intent* as they *harness varied perspectives*. The circuitous loops convey the synergy of the constructive process as it captivates participants over *expanded time and space.* Eventually, they may coalesce around a newly constructed idea, or they may have lingering differences in thinking. Either way, the compelling nature of the process ensures participants leave the conversation with thinking that's deepened and changed. Each carries footprints of others' thinking with them, enabling bits of the conversation to resonate internally, likely to surface again as they connect to new inquiries.

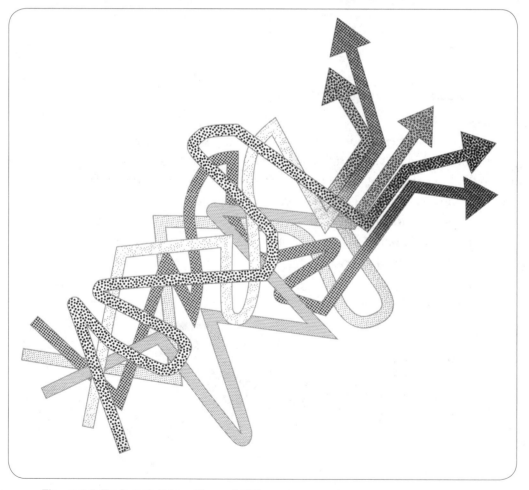

Figure 1.5 The Dynamic Nature of Purposeful Talk

Purposeful Talk in the Classroom

All of this brings us back to Dominic, Luis, and Ana, and their efforts to understand the minds and motives of the German and Allied soldiers on that Christmas Eve so long ago. As Luis asserted, "we gotta get more thinking. 'Cuz we—all of us—think it's messed up!"

I looked up into the three faces as they gathered around, knowing I had no answers for them. But these three weren't looking for answers. Rather, they were in search of ideas. When Luis comments, "Yeah, we gotta get more thinking," he highlights their *constructive intent*—a quest to incorporate new thoughts into an evolving process.

His addition of, "'Cuz we—all of us—think it's messed up!" underscores the realization that they might be stuck because they all see the soldiers' behavior in the same way—illogical, or "messed up." They were searching for *varied perspectives*, and Dominic sensed possibility when I happened through the door. Clearly, my designation as old*er* (as opposed to simply old . . . or so I keep telling myself) made me a candidate for that much-needed perspective.

Dominic, Luis, and Ana's conversation, I later discovered, had already spanned *extended time and space* when I happened through the classroom door. The compelling nature of the ideas created a dynamic process that had started days ago as the three questioned, wrestled with tentativeness, and deliberately sought the range of perspectives needed to deepen and broaden their thinking. They carried their tentative thoughts home and back again, reengaged each day with conversational openings such as, "I asked my grandma and she said . . . ," or "My dad thinks. . . ."

The expanded time proved very supportive for Ana, a quiet contemplator who didn't utter a word in our opening excerpt. Interestingly, it was Ana who eventually offered a pivotal insight. I visited the group several days later, curious about how their thinking had evolved. As we talked, Ana traced her finger along the words on the last page—the page showing soldiers hunkered back in their trenches as Christmas Eve came to a close. Ana pointed out, "The author said '*wondering*'—see, 'Back to the tren—trenches. Back to the waiting. *Wondering* what had just happened to us, and *wondering* what the next move should be.'"

Then, Ana suggested, "They don't want it [the war] now. Wondering—they're wondering! They know it's messed up, too."

Multiple reads with ample time for a mix of purposeful talk and inner contemplation enabled Ana, along with Dominic and Luis, to "get to a place that you just can't get to in one mind." These children were on the verge of constructing understandings with potential to move them from the text into the world, exploring the complexity of conflict and the dynamic nature of human relationships.

This process was possible because these children learn together daily in a classroom alive with purposeful talk. Conversations that emphasize the power of perspective as children engage daily with ideas, recognizing that thinking may begin tentatively, then deepen and strengthen as talk builds toward meaning and relevancy. A mix of curiosity, a need for clarity, intrigue, passion, and urgency drive their efforts. And a child-centered inquiry approach to learning allows them the time and space to extend their conversations and construct together.

A mix of curiosity, a need for clarity, intrigue, passion, and urgency drives their efforts. And a child-centered inquiry approach to learning allows them the time and space to extend their conversations and construct together.

Wegerif labels such classrooms "dialogic classrooms," defining them as places where teachers engage children in processes for learning *about* talk and *through* talk simultaneously (2013, 16). In these classrooms, teachers immerse children like Dominic, Luis, and Ana in teaching and learning focused on strengthening the talk they use as they construct their thinking. A deep understanding of purposeful talk becomes their North Star, guiding decisions about how to engage children in talk, and why. Holding true to this North Star matters, because, as Yogi Berra so eloquently stated, "If you don't know where you're going, you might not get there" (2002, 52).

If you want to go fast,

go alone.

If you want to go far,

go together.

—African proverb

Two

A Place for Purposeful Talk to Thrive

A Snapshot of Purposeful Talk

I am settled on the carpet with my second and third graders, immersed in ideas nudged open by Martin Waddell's *A Kitten Called Moonlight* (2001). This gentle tale invites readers alongside a mother and daughter as they share yet another retelling of a favorite story—that of the moonlit evening a stray kitten wandered into their lives. We've read the last page and tied up our ideas . . . or so I think. As I attempt to transition the group to independent reading, Lawrence, who had hovered on the edge of our conversation, stops me. "But . . ." he queries, a pensive look on his face, "Why did they tell it again?"

Throughout the read-aloud, the children had been making sense of the mother and daughter's retelling of their story and the closeness that this ritual created, but clearly not to Lawrence's satisfaction. Tentative thinking still swirls in his mind, and he needs more time to talk.

Curious, I eye the circle, wanting to see how—or if—the others might pick up this thread and rework it. Recognizing that I am not going to step in, Eric takes up Lawrence's query.

Eric: Families really do it. So they remember their good times.

Brenda: Yeah—because my family does it.

Kendra: Telling stuff? What . . .

Brenda: [Picking up the line of thinking before Kendra is able to finish her question] My mom—she tells about how when we're little—the stuff we did.

Eric: Yeah—so you can remember it.

Rosa: And so they—all of them knows it's special together.

Jamika: Yeah—see [pointing toward the book]. On the cover—how they are when they tell it.

Rosa: Yeah—special. It's how the mom and the girl are together.

I look to Lawrence and, with a tilt of my head, invite his thoughts. Still pensive, Lawrence simply nods. I am torn. I know he is intently thinking. I wonder, should I push him to vocalize his thoughts, tentative as they may be, or allow him to wrestle with them a bit more on his own? Do I back the group up to Rosa's thinking and ask her to elaborate, building on her notion about the potential of a shared story? Or do I nudge at Eric's idea that this is something families do, questioning in a way that might move the thinking to other contexts where shared story creates bonds? Do we tackle all of this now, or revisit the thinking tomorrow, allowing Lawrence—and the others—time and space to mull things over? Or one better, do I hand the book to Lawrence, knowing that his community will rally around him, supporting his journey?

As I ponder these teaching moves, I am struck not only by Lawrence's keen focus on his own developing understanding, but also on the response of his learning community. Lawrence didn't press pause on my efforts to move the group along because a classroom chart or protocol demanded it. Although mostly silent on the outside, he was fully captivated by the ideas that had been building among the group, and those still swirling in his mind. His need to understand propelled his query, which his classmates recognized as a serious attempt to wrestle with meaning. They responded with sincerity and constructive intent, offering both tentative beginnings and a range of perspectives as they fully reengaged alongside him.

A Place for Purposeful Talk to Thrive

On this morning, Lawrence and his classmates inhabited what Rupert Wegerif refers to as "dialogic space" (2016). Dialogic space is a metaphor for the shared, dynamic space of meaning that opens up between or among participants in a dialogue. It forms as we immerse fully with thoughts that compel us, wrestle with the tug of varied perspectives, and construct unexpected new ideas with others.

When children are in the metaphorical "dialogic space," their constructive process is surrounded by shared beliefs about the importance of their work together, and the value of every voice. Because they respect and value each other, they're able to bring themselves and their lived experiences into the process. Valuing all voices helps children to dig into ideas with depth and honesty, leading to more extended talk. In this way, learning communities put talk to work, and the work of talk creates social bonds that continually strengthen the community. As Peter Senge explains it:

> A unique relationship develops among team members who enter into dialogue regularly. They develop a deep trust that cannot help but carry over to discussions. They develop a richer understanding of the uniqueness of each person's point of view. They experience how larger understandings emerge by holding one's own point of view "gently." (1990, 248)

Figure 2.1 adds the thread of a strong learning community to the dynamic work of constructing through talk, emphasizing the ways community develops with and supports the process.

Simon Sinek defines such communities as, "a group of people who agree to grow together" (@simonsinek, July 30, 2018). Agreement implies a willingness to coalesce as a group and grow collaboratively, but agreement doesn't just happen, and it certainly can't be mandated. As teachers, we have to nurture the conditions that lead children like Lawrence and his classmates to *agree* to grow together and form a community that thinks and talks well together.

> *Valuing all voices helps children to dig into ideas with depth and honesty, leading to more extended talk.*

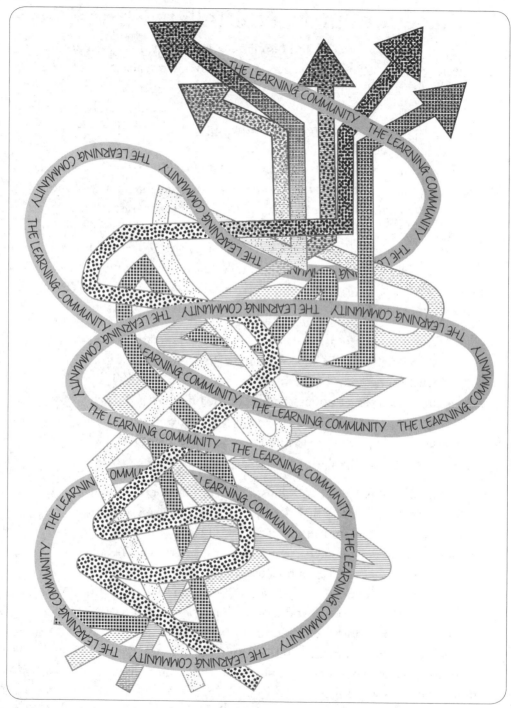

Figure 2.1 The Critical Support of a Strong Learning Community

In this chapter, we'll explore two critical conditions for transforming classrooms into powerful learning communities capable of "dialogic space": supporting children as they engage with each other, and supporting children as they engage with ideas. These conditions create communities where children build shared and individual learning identities. Communities where they can be brave. Communities where purposeful talk thrives.

> **Essentially, learning communities put talk to work, and the work of talk creates social bonds that continually strengthen the community.**

Engaging with Each Other

Learning is a collective social practice. It's dynamic, joyful, full of surprises, and by nature, it's *relational*. Peter Johnston reminds us, "The social relationships within which [children] learn are a part of their learning" (2012b, 65). To learn together, children need to figure out how to live in the confined space of a classroom, developing processes that enable them to navigate their environment, and each other, with care, respect and trust. But this can be a challenge. We've all experienced those frustrating times when we planned for children to engage in conversations and projects, but we ended up with what Robin Alexander refers to as "the seeming paradox of students working everywhere in groups but rarely *as* groups" (2004, 14).

The key is that we can't just plan for children to engage with each other in thoughtful ways and expect it to happen; we have to develop and nurture the relationships that lead to the sort of collective effort we saw with Lawrence and his classmates. We must remember that as children navigate their daily life together, they're creating the story of who they are, individually and collectively. This evolving story shapes the way they feel in the classroom space. It's this feeling, this story, that builds communities that are poised to think and talk well together. With this conversation as a model, let's consider now a few ways you can help children build learning communities in which they engage thoughtfully with each other, as these children did when Lawrence pushed pause and asked, "But . . . why?"

> **To learn together, children need to figure out how to live in the confined space of a classroom, developing processes that enable them to navigate their environment, and each other, with care, respect and trust.**

Embrace Rituals and Routines

Out of both necessity and habit, people who live together in the same space for any length of time develop rituals and routines that help them move through life together. This is as true in our classrooms as it is in our homes. Think about your own classroom. What are your routines for, say, the end of the day? How did they evolve? Are they the same this year as they were last? Are they the same as the classroom next door to yours? In all likelihood, the *particular* way you end the school day with this group of children in this school year is unique in at least some ways. Knowing the routines for dismissal in this one *particular* classroom is what makes children feel like insiders, an important feeling of community. Rituals are important, too, of course—the insider ways we celebrate birthdays, finish a good chapter book read aloud, mourn for lost teeth, or greet each other in the morning.

Developing and nurturing rituals and routines together *with* children is one of the simplest ways we can build a feeling of community in our classrooms—and they were certainly powerful in Lawrence's classroom. Over time, he and his classmates developed ways of being together as individual and collective needs emerged, shared goals developed, and respect and trust grew. Most of the class rituals began as simple acts with joyful and powerful impact. One heartfelt example was the passing of a box of tissues at the first inkling of sadness in a read-aloud text. This ritual started when Elaina grabbed a tissue for herself as we sniffled our way through a read-aloud of *The Doorman* by Edward Grimm (2000). Elaina compassionately handed the box over to the next student in the circle, who handed it to the next, who handed it to the next . . . and around the circle it went. This process was repeated a week or so later, midway into Mem Fox's *Wilfred Gordon McDonald Partridge* (1989), as the children noted a catch in my voice (that page about the big brother going off to war tugs at my heart every time). This passing of the tissue box occurred over and over, any time we settled in to read a text with a title or cover illustration that hinted toward being a tearjerker. The ritual eventually spawned a category of texts that had an honored place in the classroom library: tissue-box books.

The children in Lawrence's class shared many other "insider" rituals—ways of settling in and greeting each other in the morning, silly ways of walking up and down the ramp to the classroom, ways of passing materials, and on and on. None of these were my doing. They sprang up authentically as the children figured out how to be together, and love and honor who they were individually and collectively. The stories of how the rituals evolved became almost as important as the rituals themselves, and the children loved sharing them with confused classroom guests, using them to invite these guests into the community.

Speak Insider's Language

Language itself is another powerful way to bond a community. Expressions become inside jokes, funny only to those with an insider's status. These expressions become both ritual and affirmations of belonging. In this class, "That blew my sox off!" was a favorite, and it seemed to find its way into conversations any time characters—or classmates—surprised or amazed, always followed by winks and giggles. Sometimes, the insider's language in a community is serious, too, with code words to indicate that someone just needs a little space for himself, or an expression children use to let their classmates know that they need help.

The particular ways you and your children use language as you move through the day are all powerful markers of what make you *you*—a classroom community like no other. The more you support the development of this shared language, the more likely children are to use it to engage with one another as beings that belong together.

Gather in Meaningful Ways

Margaret Wheatley writes, "Circles create soothing space, where even reticent people can realize that their voice is welcome" (2010, 238). In this spirit, class meetings are a powerful tool for bringing the community together to think and talk about important aspects of classroom life. Lawrence and his classmates were as apt to request a meeting as I was, and we used them to celebrate, problem-solve, and plan. One particularly joyful example is a meeting the class requested to address an issue they were having with library access. The children took books from our classroom library home to enjoy with their families. Many had younger siblings who reveled in their choices, and they wanted these siblings to share in the joy of selecting texts. So, together they dreamed up the perfect solution: opening the classroom door a bit earlier one day a week so families could spend a few minutes in our library together. By the time they sat me down to discuss their proposal, they had prepared a presentation that included counterarguments in case I protested. Protest? Seriously?

Dedicating instructional time for meetings to talk about and explore community issues sends an important message. Too often in classrooms, children aren't consulted when problems arise or issues need to be addressed. The adult in the room decides what to do, and children comply. But if we want children to talk together well about big, important ideas, we have to also honor their talk and insights about seemingly smaller matters of daily classroom life. When children know that their agendas will be taken seriously—that they have the right to *call* a meeting—they understand that their voices, both individually and collectively, are truly valued in the community space.

Co-Create Shared Norms

Norms are different than routines, and the difference is significant, particularly for talk. We use routines to manage things that happen basically the same way every time. If we applied routines to our talk, we would create an inauthentic sameness to our conversations that is the antithesis to the dynamic nature of purposeful talk. Many protocols and checklists for classroom talk have this exact effect. Norms, on the other hand, are socially developed constructs that help us manage in situations that are familiar, but, by nature, unpredictable. Norms help us know how to interact at a party, for instance, or how to move through a crowd exiting a theatre. Different groups of people in different families, workspaces, cultures, and the like may have different norms for the same kinds of situations. This is why establishing norms *together* in a classroom is a powerful tool for community building.

Norms are guides, not rules, and the more experience we have in particular situations, the more we understand the subtleties of that guidance. For this reason, it's important that the norms you establish for interactions like purposeful talk are developed over time as your children grow together. In Figure 2.2 you see a chart that Lawrence and his classmates co-created as they grew to understand the potential of purposeful talk, and ways of thinking and talking together that helped them to harness that potential.

The chart was a living document in the classroom, growing and changing as children's understanding of and ability with purposeful talk grew. If and when talk wobbled, we tackled the wobble together and added new thoughts and solutions to our repertoire. The children took ownership of the chart, adding suggestions on sticky notes as they worked together throughout the day.

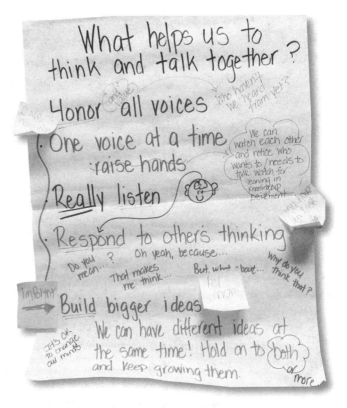

Figure 2.2 Norms for Purposeful Talk

Engaging with Ideas

Developing strong learning relationships is necessary, but not sufficient to ensure communities will passionately engage and pursue meaning, perhaps to the point of becoming captivated. There's another factor at play. Children also need to know that they're pulling together to do things of significance—things that matter in the world. In literacy pursuits, that means time with texts filled with compelling ideas worth talking about—ideas that connect with children's minds and touch their hearts.

Compelling texts, such as *A Kitten Called Moonlight*, are often ripe with ambiguity, open to multiple interpretations, and resist closure. They launch ideas that matter to children, and abound with characters that are relatable, complex, and imperfect, with all-too-human struggles. They touch the heart as well as the mind and offer fodder for thinking about the world beyond the text. Engaging with compelling and complex ideas,

> *Children also need to know that they're pulling together to do things of significance— things that matter in the world.*

Douglas Barnes tells us, "facilitates learning which is active and which prepares young people for a complex world with many uncertainties" (2010, 7). Once again, using the conversation about this book as a model, let's now consider four ways we can work to make sure children have access to ideas that powerfully engage them.

Access to Compelling Texts

As Matt de la Peña notes, "Books are tools for conversation" (2018). Given this, the kinds of books we fill our classrooms with matter. Books that bellow, books that gently beacon, books that evoke a smile, a smirk, or a furrowed brow. A range of books to compel our incredible range of readers.

In a seminal study of engaged reading, Ivey and Johnston found that texts are most compelling when they explore ideas that are relevant to children's lives (2017). Relevant ideas captivate, moving readers from silent contemplation to brave conversation. It's important to note that relevancy is often less about the literal text and more about the broader ideas the text opens. Lawrence's puzzlement wasn't about a mother and daughter and a found kitten. Rather, he was deeply touched by, and puzzled by, rituals that bond people—the ritual of the two characters, and then of those of his classmates and their families.

Texts that touch upon edgy ideas or complex issues actively compel (Ivey and Johnston 2010). Although our tendency may be to shy away from edgy materials, the truth is that these texts often touch on issues that are very real and relevant to children's lived experiences. Children are eager to dive in, using the guise of fictional characters, settings, and plots to make sense of their world.

Young adult literature has led the way in this realization, with texts like Angie Thomas' *The Hate U Give* (2018) or Jason Reynolds' *Long Way Down* (2017) captivating teens and adults alike. These texts may provide a safe context for sorting through experiences that mirror children's own lives, or help them to build empathy for people whose lived experiences may differ from their own. Similarly, delicately edgy picture books abound to captivate our younger learners. Gently crafted, these texts invite questions and propel talk that nudges open wondering and awareness about very real ideas. Texts like Margriet Ruurs' *Stepping Stones: A Refugee Family's Journey* (2016) and Francesca Sanna's *The Journey* (2016) offer opportunities for children to engage with the voices of people braving unthinkable challenges. Trudy Ludwig's *The Invisible Boy* (2013) and Jacqueline Woodson's *Each Kindness* (2012) offer the opportunity to reflect, think, and talk about our role in others' well-being. And Katherine Applegate's *Ivan: The Remarkable True Story of the Shopping Mall Gorilla* (2014), Lynn Cherry's *The Great Kapok Tree* (1990), and Yukio Tsuchiya's *The Faithful Elephants: A True Story of Animals, People, and War* (1997) beg for conversations about human responsibility.

These are the kinds of texts that propelled our read-aloud time and filled the classroom library. Lawrence and his classmates were thinking and talking about ideas that mattered in their lives, ideas that helped them make sense of their world, and ideas that helped them to envision the myriad of ways their voices and actions mattered. However, as Lawrence so keenly illustrates, ideas don't have to be edgy to compel. They just need to tug at hearts, perplex and stretch the mind, and capture the imagination. Engagement with these ideas can be seen, felt and heard. We see engagement when children are absorbed in silent contemplation. We hear it in their earnestness, and we feel it through the tempo and intensity of their talk.

As you think ahead about what you might read aloud, be sure to ask the question, *Are there ideas in this book* worth *talking about? Ideas that will matter to* this group *of children?*

Shift from Answers to Ideas

One of the biggest impediments to engaging with ideas, even the most compelling, is an overarching emphasis on answers. When children believe reading is a process of finding answers inside their own minds, they see no need to think and talk with other readers. A focus on answers also creates a right-wrong mindset, shutting down children's willingness to explore a range of ideas.

To understand how this happens, we'll need to step out of Lawrence's classroom and examine a bit of talk from a first-grade class reading Audrey Penn's *A Pocket Full of Kisses* (2006). This talk will help to contrast an emphasis on answers with an emphasis on ideas, and it also brings the role of the teacher into the equation. *A Pocket Full of Kisses* is the delightful story of Chester, a young raccoon learning to share his mother's love (and kisses) with an even younger sibling. This text usually sets children to wrestling with a range of very human—and very relevant—emotions and behaviors. But in this particular conversation, these compelling ideas never emerge. Clues as to why are embedded in this snippet as the children move from partner talk back to whole-group conversation:

> **Teacher:** Look [at the illustration] to see how Chester feels. Who can tell me how Chester feels? Liana? What did you tell your partner?
>
> **Liana:** He's sad.
>
> **Teacher:** Yes! Sad—he's sad. What's making him sad? Conner?
>
> **Conner:** It's 'cuz she [the mother] gave the kisses to him [baby brother], and he's [Chester] sad. He wants the kisses.
>
> **Teacher:** [Nodding] Why does mom give kisses to his brother? Amanda?
>
> **Amanda:** She loves him, too. He [Chester] can have kisses, too. He—he—he's gotta ask to get some.
>
> **Teacher:** [Nodding again] Will that make Chester feel better?
>
> **Multiple voices:** Yes!
>
> **Teacher:** Good. Let's see what happens . . .

Let's unpack what's happening here, beginning with the teacher's prompting of Liana. When she asks, "Who can tell *me* . . . ?" she indicates that the purpose of talk is telling an answer, and specifically, telling that answer to the teacher. The teacher's confirmation of Liana's response indicates that there indeed was a single right answer, and Liana nailed it—no further talk needed. A follow-up question is directed to Conner, who also gives the anticipated answer to the teacher, as evidenced by the teacher's nodding.

So what's behind this? Many of us were apprenticed as students into a well-documented, inauthentic pattern of talk, widely known as Initiate/Respond/Evaluate (IRE). IRE positions the teacher authoritatively, focusing effort on predetermined answers to often predetermined questions, as opposed to focusing authentically and responsively on constructing ideas (Mehan, 1979). This pattern of talk is very specific to school. And, despite our best efforts, it still creeps back into our practice.

By emphasizing the construction of ideas as children think and talk purposefully, we create what Douglas Barnes describes as "the antithesis to 'right answerism'" (2010, 7). Let's consider a few unexplored possibilities that might have emerged if these children had been pursuing ideas as opposed to telling answers. Could Chester also be jealous? Annoyed? Angry? What are his fears? What will become of his relationship with his mother? With his new sibling?

What insights into Chester, themselves, each other, and ultimately their world might the children have developed? How could that constructive process have strengthened their learning community? And what effect would that have on engagement? The bottom line is that if we want children to explore ideas, we need to let go of expectations of a single correct response, and open space for them to engage strategically together.

Linger with Ideas Inside Texts

Thomas Newkirk reminds us that reading is not a race. He cautions, "Take your time. Pay attention. Touch the words and tell me how they touch you" (2012, 197). Compelling, complex texts contain layers of meaning and relevancy, and exploring them takes time. Lawrence's question and his classmates' willingness to reengage with him makes it clear that they were willing to slow down, to linger with ideas. They had no expectation of a single answer. Nor did they have a sense of finality to their thinking. Knowing this about them, and knowing Lawrence as a learner, I decided to hand *A Kitten Called Moonlight* off to him as we settled into reading workshop that morning.

Sure enough, as Lawrence settled in, Brenda, Kaya, and Issy made their way over to join him. Others stopped in at different times to listen or add a thought. I deliberately hung back, giving them time to find their way. When I finally checked in, the children were lingering over the last two pages, where Waddell hints at the power of shared story by leaving the reader lingering on Charlotte and Mommy's words:

"We love that story, don't we Moonlight?"
Charlotte said.
"And I know why," said Mommy.
"We love it because it's about us,"
Charlotte said. "Moonlight,
And Mommy and me." (Waddell 2001)

Hearing new questions and room in their talk for thinking to grow, I decided to return to these same last two pages during read-aloud the next day. I reread, and then turned from the text to the children, my own question at the ready. But Kaya was also ready.

Kaya: Yeah—that's the part we talked about—me and Lawrence.

Issy: And me!

Kaya: Uh huh—and it said *us*—the mommy and girl. And Brenda said for her family, too—

Brenda: Yeah—my mom and us.

Maria: So, Kaya, what do you think's going on?

Kaya: It's specialness—they tell it so they can know. And they can feel it.

Maria: Brenda, does that fit with what your family does?

Brenda: My brother, he lives far. He had to go. He calls and my mom—she tells him the stories sometimes.

Anthony: On the phone?

Brenda: [Nodding her head in agreement] And they laugh. But sometimes she cries a little bit.

Maria: Oh—why?

Laura: Maybe because he's far away . . .

The children were hovering on the edge of a deeper understanding, a realization that story bonds us not only in the moment, but also across space and time. They weren't there—not quite yet, but the ideas they were exploring in *A Kitten Called Moonlight* resonated across time, resurfacing in later inquiries, class meetings, and small conversations. Each time, their thinking was reshaped by new contexts and ideas, and they continued to propel a process of understanding.

When readers have extended time to engage and construct meaning, as these children did, a range of perspectives typically emerges that serve to deepen and broaden their thinking. As Douglas Barnes notes, when children first begin to explore, their thinking, and hence their talk, is often tentative. This tentativeness is critical to the constructive process. Barnes refers to it as "exploratory talk," explaining that exploratory talk "provides a ready tool for trying out different ways of thinking and understanding" (1992, 28).

But over time, as children explore ideas from varied perspectives, their talk may begin taking a more critical angle. This progression occurs as they agree and disagree, challenge one another's thinking, and negotiate between and among differences. Far from being counterproductive, critical talk strengthens lines of thinking and enables children to construct informed points of view. Given time, initially tentative ideas transform into more composed thought (Barnes 2008, 5). This is evidenced by an increased eloquence to children's talk, which Barnes refers to as "presentational talk."

When we revisit a text, we offer children time to linger with ideas and to move from tentative thought to more polished thought. This may happen across two or more sequential days, as with *A Kitten Called Moonlight*. Or we might cycle back to a text when the ideas we're exploring elsewhere have the potential to bump up alongside a conversation in intriguing ways. Too, at some point, the children themselves may make a connection and request we revisit a text—or revisit it on their own. Whatever causes us to revisit a text, just remember that revisiting is not the same as reteaching. We don't delve back into a text to reinforce current understanding. Rather, it's an opportunity to slow down and reenter the dialogic space to deepen the construction of meaning. Revisiting doesn't necessarily mean rereading the entirety of a text. Rather, we tap into children's questions, confusions, and intrigue, cycling back to portions of the text that seem most powerful.

Pursue Ideas Across Texts

Finally, remember that compelling texts offer up ideas that are almost always bigger than a single text alone. Learning how to explore ideas across multiple sources and from different authors' perspectives is pivotal to developing children's sense of what it means to understand with breadth and depth (Nichols 2009). This process again slows down the meaning making as children tussle with differences in thinking or new angles on ideas.

For example, there's incredible potential to deepen and broaden the ideas Lawrence and his classmates explored in *A Kitten Called Moonlight* by reading other texts with subtle differences and varied angles on relationships, rituals that bond, and the importance of those bonds. Patricia Polacco, for instance, has written extensively about her family traditions—many of which transcend generations. Or, texts like *Drawn Together*, by Minh Lê (2018), may broaden childrens' thinking as they consider the ways tools other than words help to forge bonds that bridge cultural and language gaps. Texts like *An Angel for Solomon Singer*, by Cynthia Rylant (1996), may push thinking even further as children empathize with those who lack social bonds and imagine what role these might play in their lives.

When we open conversations to a greater range of perspectives, we're bound to spark a little controversy now and again, but as we noted earlier, controversy has great potential to strengthen engagement and talk. Rupert Wegerif points out that dialogue is at its best when there is a "gap or difference between voices" (2013, 29). Where there's dissonance, children need to talk purposefully. As they draw from the strength of their community for support, their constructive process tightens the bonds.

Uptake: The Powerful Outcome of Engaging with Each Other and with Ideas

When Lawrence halted the transition to independent reading, his classmates could have responded with rolling eyes, sighs, or cries of "We just talked about that!" They could have—but they didn't. Instead, they recognized his question as an invitation. Lawrence trusted his community and reached out, and his classmates took him seriously. Their response was genuine, thoughtful, and collaborative.

Throughout this bit of talk, we see evidence of what Martin Nystrand calls "uptake." Uptake refers to the process of taking in, responding to, and growing someone else's thinking (1997, 73). Uptake is a powerful process that becomes possible only when children engage thoughtfully with each other and with compelling ideas. It requires openness to having another's thinking affect one's own.

Lawrence displays uptake-readiness when he eagerly invites his classmates' thinking with his question. Eric exhibits uptake as he takes Lawrence's question in, and genuinely responds. The way their thoughts build is added evidence of uptake, as is Brenda's anticipation of the whole of Kendra's question. Because of their skillful uptake, the children know they've been listened to and their thoughts have been valued—critical components in engaging through purposeful talk and in strengthening the learning community.

In strong communities, children are encouraged and supported to bring their lived experiences into the mix, offering them as added context to push meaning making. Uptake enables children to build on the potential of this. As Lawrence and his classmates talk, Brenda brings her family experiences into the process, which intrigues Kendra, who asks for more information. Eric imagines himself into Brenda's mom's mind, and offers his own explanation for her actions. Rosa then extends that imagining to the whole of Brenda's family.

This genuine honoring of voices, respect for individual inquiries, and recognition of the power of the collective is only possible in a strong learning community. Without the desire and skill to engage with each other, children lose the constructive potential of multiple voices, varied perspectives, and the power of the collective to deepen and extend conversations.

As you consider creating a place for talk to thrive in your own classroom, remember that if children are to develop as a learning community, they must believe that their efforts to engage with each other and with ideas *matter*. They need to connect what they are doing with a real *why*—the development of purposefully literate lives. And they need to see that purposefully literate lives are at the same time both individual and social. When children set about real work in real ways, and feel the support of their community alongside them, the learning becomes their own, and they *agree* to grow together.

> **Without the desire and skill to engage with each other, children lose the constructive potential of multiple voices, varied perspectives, and the power of the collective to deepen and extend conversations.**

Teaching requires

constant improvisation.

It is jazz.

—Peter Johnston

Three

A Process for Teaching Purposeful Talk

A Snapshot of Purposeful Talk

I'm settled with a lively group of fourth graders, reading Laban Carrick Hill's *Dave the Potter: Artist, Poet, Slave* (2010). Set in South Carolina in the 1800s, this stunning text positions readers alongside enslaved artisan David Drake as he skillfully works his clay. As the children think and talk about the sparse, lyrical text, the vivid collages adding depth to Dave's story, and bits of prior knowledge, their conversation is a passionate mix of awe and ire. As we reach the end, the children are grappling with the bold poetry Dave inscribed on his pots. Confused, their talk decidedly slows. Out of the corner of my eye, I notice Jaylen's frustration.

> **Maria:** Jaylen, what's going on over there? You're shaking your head.
>
> **Jaylen:** Well—I don't get—the words are weird. Why did he put them [the poems] on it?
>
> **Ellie:** On the pots?
>
> **Multiple voices:** Yeah . . . I don't get why . . . me, too . . .

Scanning the group, I see faces scrunched in thought, noses wrinkled, heads shaking, eyes darting about the circle, hoping others might offer insight. *They're stuck*, I think.

I wait, anticipating tentative thoughts, an inkling of an idea. Sensing none, I suggest a turn and talk. As partners lean in together, I move about the pairs and trios—listening, questioning, nudging. It's slow going at first. Several partners gesture toward the text, asking to revisit specific pages. Others prompt each other with questions and tentative theories. Some are trying to understand Dave's poems, and others, his motives for writing them. I listen for intriguing thoughts, and find a possibility with Emilio and Kiley.

As the class gathers back together, Emilio shares the struggle he and Kiley were having with a passage that hints at Dave's motive: "But to Dave, it was a pot large enough to store a season's grain harvest, to put up salted meat, to hold memories." As Emilio explains, Cole chimes in:

> **Cole:** We didn't get that, too—when it said he put in the meat and the memories.
>
> **Kiley:** We—yeah, we still don't get about the meat. But I said, the memories, I said it's, like, poems—it's the memories. It's why he did it.

Ahh . . . a potential foothold. Slowly, the children's ability with talk is nudging meaning making forward. But, there is more confusion, and Mayesha leans in to clarify.

> **Mayesha:** I don't get—the poems—do you mean the poems—that's the memories?
>
> **Kiley:** Well, yeah. It's *his* memories. Maybe to remember his family—so he doesn't forget because he can't see them.

Mayesha's head tilts as she looks quizzically at Kiley. She starts to speak, but then takes an audible breathe as she formulates her words. Her classmates, reading her intent to say more, hold off.

> **Mayesha:** But he—he doesn't tell about them [his family].
>
> **Maria:** [Looking around the circle] What do you all think?
>
> **Francisco:** Oh yeah—it could make him remember, you know, when he thinks so he can write the poems, he remembers and maybe it feels good to him.

As Francisco's thinking sinks in, I look around the circle and again see furrowed brows and pursed lips. Jax leans in as if to speak, then catches her breathe, and sits back to think some more. The book is open to an illustration of Dave, alone, bent over his potter's wheel. Courtney studies it quizzically, as if waiting for Dave to look up, smile, and speak. Then, a head of shaking curls catches my attention. It's Shawn, who draws from a line on the last page to exuberantly propose a counter theory.

Shawn: But—no, I think—it said "us" . . . to let *us* know!

And with that, a chorus of "Ohhhhhs!" and "Whats?" erupts. Jaylen, whose confusion launched the journey into Dave's possible motives, throws up her arms as if to embrace newfound clarity. We reread the last page—"but before the jar completely hardened, Dave picked up a stick and wrote to let us know he was here." Voices clamor to be heard all at once, prompting another turn and talk. Unsure where to listen in first, I hold back to survey faces and gestures, and revel in the growing excitement.

A Process for Teaching Purposeful Talk

In classrooms where children use purposeful talk to wrestle with big ideas, each question, each tentative thought has the potential to launch conversations as rich and varied as the range of voices involved. These conversations, like the one in this snapshot, move to a rhythm driven by the meaning-making process itself. When ideas are connecting, the pace quickens and the energy becomes palpable and visible. Talk is punctuated with bursts of "Oh!" and "Yeah!" Inevitably though, new understandings yield to new questions, and these constructive highs are followed by contemplative lulls as children think and search for words to voice tentative possibilities. Then, gradually, a new idea emerges, leading to another, and another—and the pace quickens again as understanding evolves.

As this group of children so beautifully illustrates, thinking and talking to understand is not a linear march through the pages of a text. Their conversation was richly dynamic, mov-

> *In classrooms where children use purposeful talk to wrestle with big ideas, each question, each tentative thought has the potential to launch conversations as rich and varied as the range of voices involved.*

ing forward and backward, in and out of the text as they engaged with ideas and with each other. Essentially, it mirrored the squiggly "this is what it really looks like" line in our dialogic process image from Chapter One (see Figure 1.2, page 10). An intense need to understand propelled the children, as well as an array of talk behaviors I first introduced in *Comprehension Through Conversation* (2006). As they talked together, these children were

★   hearing all voices

★   growing ideas

★   negotiating meaning.

In this chapter, we'll consider how you might teach children to understand and use talk behaviors that help them construct stronger understandings—teaching *about* and *through* purposeful talk simultaneously. Then, the following chapters will explore the intent of these talk behaviors and delve deeper into the process of teaching purposeful talk.

Teaching that helps children learn *about* and *through* purposeful talk simultaneously is as dynamic as the talk itself. It requires, as Peter Johnston (2012b) suggests, constant improvisation—a teaching stance that promises both beauty and challenge.

The beauty, as we've been exploring, lies in the meaning making itself, the depth of understanding that becomes possible, and the bonds formed through the process. The challenge is that the uncertain, on-your-toes stance of teaching into the process can seem daunting. All too often, the uncertainty sends us scurrying for the safety of talk protocols. These protocols, complete with talking sticks, marbles, lock-step sequences, and language frames, ease our fear by offering structure. They control who can talk, what they can say, when, and how often. They teach the etiquette of discourse, instructing children to sit up straight, raise their hands, make eye contact, and disagree respectfully.

All of this may sound good and look good on the surface, but what protocols do in essence is iron out the messy, dynamic nature of constructing through talk. The resulting sense of calm and order may ease our angst, but what we sacrifice is the very messiness that encourages the tentative talk and productive struggle that leads to broad and deep thinking. Protocols set children up for compliant behavior, but they do nothing to help them build agentive identities as people who think and talk well together, or to internalize the strategies that help them to engage in purposeful talk independently.

Authentic, purposeful talk is, by nature, unpredictable, but your teaching doesn't have to be. The beauty is that, rather than protocoling the energy out of dialogic interactions, we can teach *into* the energy, lifting students' ability with talk as we strengthen their meaning making. We can teach purposeful talk by actively engaging children in a responsive, three-step process that allows us to teach *about* talk as children make meaning *through* talk. The three steps of this responsive process are the following actions:

> *We can teach purposeful talk by actively engaging children in a responsive, three-step process that allows us to teach about talk as children make meaning through talk.*

★ Gently **focus** children on aspects of purposeful talk behavior.

★ Authentically **facilitate** as children engage with ideas and with each other.

★ Clearly offer **feedback** that links purposeful talk behaviors to the process of constructing meaning.

When we teach into purposeful talk in this way, we wrap our support around children's process (Figure 3.1). This support helps children understand the purpose and power of their own talk and builds an agentive stance toward talk.

The key to meeting the challenges of dynamic, improvisational teaching is making **focus, facilitate,** and **feedback** a familiar cycle. Let's explore each step of this process now, and then later in Chapters Four, Five, and Six, we'll use the process to consider how you might teach each of the specific talk behaviors more intentionally.

Gently Focus

Knowing that all learning floats on a sea of talk, focusing children on talk behaviors can and should happen throughout each day, every day. Basically, any time children are talking with each other, you have an opportunity to help them get better at using their talk behaviors more

Figure 3.1 The Focus, Facilitate, Feedback Cycle

purposefully. The first step is developing awareness through an invitation to focus on an aspect of their talk behavior. An invitation might sound something like this:

> We know listening is an important part of growing ideas. As we think and talk together today, let's all try to be aware of our listening. If you realize someone's words slipped past you, be sure to ask them to repeat their thinking.

Or you might offer a little more detail, and it would sound something like this:

> As we were talking yesterday, we were starting to bounce from thought to thought without digging in. That made it harder to grow our thinking. When someone adds their voice to our conversation today, let's make sure we pause, dig into their thought, and work to grow it before we move on to different thinking.

Notice that in both cases, the focus is specific and also strategic—the framing helps children anticipate how the focus might play out for them in the actual conversation, and it gives them a strategy to address it. The purpose of focusing in this way is not to limit children to a single talk behavior at a time. Rather, the purpose of focusing on an aspect of talk behavior is simply to bring mindfulness to their dialogic efforts. A focus invites children to pay attention to their talk, and reminds them of the ways a specific behavior can support their constructive process.

> *The purpose of focusing on an aspect of talk behavior is simply to bring mindfulness to their dialogic efforts.*

Decisions about a potential talk focus, such as attention to listening, should spring from observations you make as children are engaged in talk. What do you see they need? For example, as the fourth graders talked their way through the portion of *Dave the Potter* shared at the opening of this chapter, I realized that I was the only one picking up on the scrunched faces and shaking heads. For children to think and talk productively together, it's critical that they learn to tune in to nonverbal cues, as these cues may suggest a classmate's confusion, a burning question, or an attempt to enter a conversation. If children are not attending to these cues, then this would be an important talk focus.

Of course, a talk focus helps children as they learn *about* talk, but they also need to learn *through* talk, so conversations about talk behaviors can and should dovetail with conversations about the meaning-making strategies children need to help them construct understanding. Focusing on both in tandem helps children become increasingly strategic, strengthens their understanding of meaning making as an active and social process, and emphasizes talk as a tool for engaging purposefully with each other in that process.

Authentically Facilitate

Facilitation of talk differs from traditional, teacher driven instruction as it does not attempt to corral children's process or funnel their thinking. Rather, facilitating means letting go of scripted lessons and questions, and making space for children to engage in an honest flow of talk and meaning making. A quick look back at the conversation snapshot that opened this chapter will help you understand what *facilitation* looks like in action. When I am facilitating, I'm engaged in two inquiries at once. I pay close attention to the meaning children are constructing and inquire alongside them, but I'm also studying how talk is supporting that process—or not. Based on what I'm learning as the talk unfolds, I nudge, guide, and scaffold talk, as opposed to controlling it. As Adam Kahane, author of *Solving Tough Problems*, shares, "the job of a facilitator is to help the participants speak up, listen up, and bring all of their personal resources to the work at hand" (2007, 89).

> "When I am facilitating, I'm engaged in two inquiries at once. I pay close attention to the meaning children are constructing and inquire alongside them, but I'm also studying how talk is supporting that process—or not."

Similarly, when I am facilitating, I'm also teaching students at two levels. On one level, my facilitation moves are meant to help children work together to construct broad, deep meaning from the text and the context at hand. But on the other level, my talk moves and behaviors are also teaching students how to engage with each other through talk when I'm not there—with any text and in any context. The language I use and the decisions I make show students how to engage with each other through talk, work together, and become active agents in their own learning.

With so much complexity, becoming comfortable with teaching this way is a process in and of itself. Yes, students will clamor to talk and there will be too many voices at once. No, they might not listen to each other. Quiet students will find ways to hide, while more talkative students command the airspace. I may find myself wide-eyed as students' talk is faltering, or gaining momentum, or wandering astray, wondering what to do. And, as Courtney Cazden reminds us, "Being able to hear students' ideas, to understand the sense they are making, is not as easy as it may sound" (2001, 89).

As we'll explore in Chapters Four, Five, and Six, different talk behaviors suggest different facilitation moves and language, but there are principles of facilitation that are important to keep in mind as we think about this dynamic teaching stance. Let's consider each of them briefly next.

Facilitation is Invitational

Rather than positioning the teacher as the lead talker, facilitation invites children's voices into the meaning-making process. The goal is for the teacher to become less and less important to the conversation, and for students' voices to take the lead. Invitations such as "What are you thinking?" "Is anyone wondering ___?" and "Who can build on that?" open space for tentative ideas and authentic questions and noticings to emerge, and for meaning making to genuinely build.

Facilitation is Responsive

Facilitation can't be scripted. Rather, our moves are responsive to what children say—or don't say—and the depth of meaning they are constructing—or not. When we facilitate, we take an inquiry stance, listening intently to the flow of children's talk, alert for constructive possibilities. As meaning develops, we follow where children lead. We may nudge toward specific lines of thinking to deepen and broaden them, or we may nudge toward new lines of thinking—but always in ways that honor children's thoughts, as opposed to discrediting them. And sometimes, we don't nudge at all, remembering that silence can also be a powerful and responsive facilitative move.

Facilitation is Agentive

Peter Johnston reminds us that, as teachers, our word choice "actually creates realities and invites identities" (2004, 9). Facilitative language is particularly powerful, as it speaks to relationships in the meaning-making process and lays bare our beliefs about children's capabilities. For example, consider the message we send when we say to children, "Now, who can tell *me* . . . ?" This language positions us as the all-knowing recipient of answers, and directs the limited talk to us instead of to the community. If we shift our language and ask questions such as "Is anyone curious about . . . ?" or "Maybe we should think about . . . ," we position students as capable thinkers and collaborators who construct meaning to satisfy their own intrinsic need to understand, not to please us or prove anything to us.

Facilitation is Meaning Driven

Facilitation is always focused on supporting children as they construct meaning together. We attend very closely to the ebb and flow of meaning making and tailor our facilitation to children's needs. Our work is to lightly support when meaning is flowing, and to nudge a bit more if meaning is faltering, perhaps rereading confusing parts of the text, encouraging children to notice more in a particular passage, or connecting thinking to ideas we've considered before in other conversations. Keeping meaning at the forefront, we remember that meaning making is itself agentive—if the meaning truly belongs to the children.

Clearly Offer Feedback

In the dialogic classroom, feedback spurs reflection, and helps children become aware of the depth and breadth of meaning they constructed, and the role of purposeful talk in the process.

As John Dewey reminds us, "We do not learn from experience. We learn from reflecting on an experience" (1933, 78). In the dialogic classroom, feedback spurs reflection, and helps children become aware of the depth and breadth of meaning they constructed and the role of purposeful talk in the process.

Peter Johnston uses the term *causal process feedback* to describe the kind of feedback that notices and names what children are doing, and links their actions to a specific outcome. "You did this, so that happened . . ." (2012b, 31). Causal process feedback does not involve judging or praising, which position the teacher as all-knowing and all-controlling. Rather, it focuses on highlighting children's strategic behavior and, through this, creates learning identities.

For example, Jaylen's willingness to voice her confusion in the form of a question led her classmates to join her as she considered Dave's poetry and his motives for writing it. If I were to offer causal process feedback on Jaylen's talk move, it might sound something like this:

> *As we were thinking and talking together today, Jaylen did something very thoughtful. She was confused, so she asked a question. That question caused us all to pause, and launched some talk that led to a theory about Dave's emotions and motives for writing poetry on his pots. Any time you feel that kind of confusion, asking a question can be very powerful.*

Notice that I first name Jaylen's question as a talk move, then I explain how it moved the thinking forward (the outcome), and finally, I generalize the move as something students might do again in another situation. This kind of feedback should be interjected either during or directly after a learning experience. Either way, the challenge is staying alert to aspects of talk that have a positive impact on meaning making, and then remembering to deliberately and specifically highlight their relationship. Of course, the ability to offer causal process feedback is directly related to our understanding of purposeful talk and the process of comprehending. The more we understand about the relationship between talk and meaning making, the more we see.

As their successes with talk and meaning making become visible, children become increasingly aware of the power of talk, their own process of thinking and talking together, and their ability to strengthen that process. They become increasingly strategic and agentive. In this way, our feedback not only positions children as people who can accomplish things by acting strategically, but also as contributing members of a learning community that values thinking and talking together.

> *As their successes with talk and meaning making become visible, children become increasingly aware of the power of talk, their own process of thinking and talking together, and their ability to strengthen that process. They become increasingly strategic and agentive.*

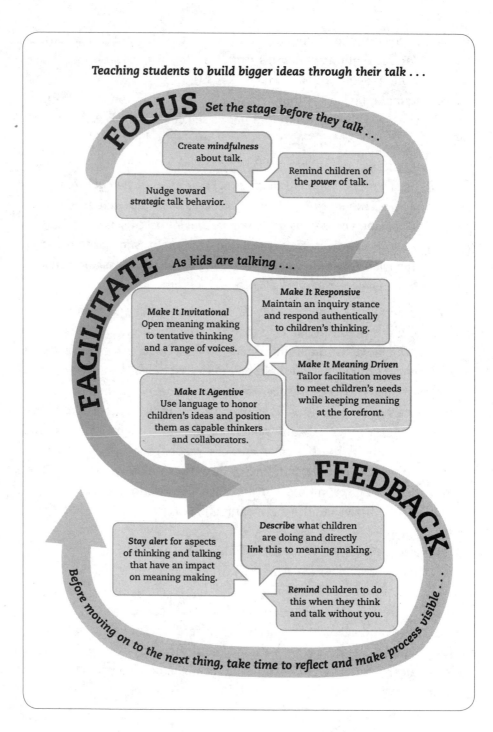

Moving from Support to Independence

As purposeful talk lifts all learning, we can use the cycle of focus, facilitation, and feedback to support children during most instructional opportunities and interactions throughout the day. It's important, however, to balance opportunities for children to talk with our support and also without it. We need to create space for children to draw from their growing understanding of purposeful talk, and engage with ideas and with each other both strategically, authentically, and independently.

Workshop structures, such as reading or writing workshop, science inquiry, or art studio, offer the perfect context for children to move seamlessly from support to independence in their engagements with talk. Workshop structures typically begin with a whole-class experience, where we can offer more supportive facilitation, and then children move out to independent work, where we can step back a bit and allow them to draw on their growing understandings of talk and meaning making as they engage in the work at hand. As the examples in this book show, I particularly utilize the flow from read-aloud to independent reading in the reading workshop to teach children *about* and *through* purposeful talk. As I engage children in this flow, there are a few key ideas I keep in mind that help me tap into the full potential of this teaching.

Read-Aloud: A Place for Support

If our hope is for children to develop communities that think and talk together, and develop richly literate lives, we need to reimagine read-alouds as places where children do most of the thinking and the talking. Read-alouds are an opportunity to read *with* children—not *to* children. Now, this may seem at odds with the idea that read-aloud is where we offer the most support for teaching purposeful talk, but it's not. We support children by selecting the text, reading the words out loud, and focusing, facilitating, and offering feedback. But, the *thinking* work is the children's—not ours. Jaylen, whose question propelled the deep conversation about *Dave the Potter*, is a poster child for children who own the thinking.

Bertrand Russell expresses so eloquently the critical importance of leaving the thinking to children, and taking their thinking seriously. Russell says:

> When you want to teach children to think, you begin by
> treating them seriously when they are little, giving them
> responsibilities, talking to them candidly, . . . and making
> them readers and thinkers of significant thoughts right
> from the beginning. That's *if* you want to teach them to
> think. (Gilbert 2018, 3)

This belief that children should own the thinking during read-aloud
sits in contrast to models that call on the teacher to determine the meaning in the text and think out loud for children, funneling them toward
that meaning. When the teacher controls the thinking, the children's role
is to comply with and build on that thinking. They may practice strategies and talk behaviors within this controlled script, but they rarely have
an opportunity to find their own importance in the text, or to become
truly strategic as they engage meaningfully with ideas and with each other.

This is not to say that we never model our thinking for children.
But it isn't our opening move. Instead, read-alouds should begin with
open-ended questions that create space for children's thinking. My first
question is always simply "What are you thinking?" If needed, I might
offer questions that nudge a bit more. "What are you thinking about this
character? Why might the character be doing that?" Modeling thinking
as the highest level of support is the last resort, used with full recognition
that we are modeling not only a strategy, but our own interpretation of
the text. It's critical to avoid any sense that our interpretation is the only
possibility. This stance perpetuates the notion of a main, big, or central
idea or theme, which creates a sense of a right answer. As we've already
explored, an emphasis on answers squelches talk. Tom Newkirk took to
the Twittersphere to push against a misguided belief in a single main idea
inside texts:

> Sometimes we talk about main idea as if it was a definite
> thing in a text—like the pit in a peach. But readers as-
> sign importance based on their intentions and their acts
> of attention. The great Roman, Seneca, said it best. There
> is nothing particularly surprising about this way which
> everyone has of deriving materials for their own individual
> interests from identical subject matter. In one and the same

meadow the cow looks for grass, the dog for the hare, and the stork for the lizard. (@Tom_Newkirk, May 14, 2018)

Newkirk's notion of finding our own importance in text echoes Louise Rosenblatt's transactional theory (1968), which views meaning making as an authentic interaction between reader and text. The key is that our efforts to focus, facilitate, and offer feedback in read-aloud, no matter how supportive, needs to honor children's thinking and meaning making as central to the process.

Reading Workshop: A Place for Independence

When children move from read-aloud to independent reading in the reading workshop, the goal is for them to take what they are learning about purposeful talk with them. But for this to happen, we have to rethink the workshop space. Reading workshop is not just about "doing independent reading." It's not just a time for children to practice their guided reading texts, or read only at their level. Nor is it time for children to sit alone in front of a screen, headphones firmly affixed, clicking their way through digital texts and text-related activities.

> *Independence is an opportunity for children to create their own learning journey, engage, struggle, strategize, adjust— and in doing so, craft agentive learning identities and richly literate lives.*

Rather, workshop should offer children an opportunity to engage in reading as a collaborative, literate pursuit. Independence is an opportunity for children to create their own learning journey, engage, struggle, strategize, adjust—and in doing so, craft agentive learning identities and richly literate lives. In this collaborative space, children learn to navigate both choice and complexity as readers. In this space, independence isn't equated with *silent* and *alone*.

Choice is a critical element in engagement. Children's choices may be loosely framed by a particular unit of study, but there needs to be ample room for them to select texts that compel, and to experience a range of authors, genres, and text types as they go. We teach them to ask questions such as:

★ *What topics, ideas and authors are beckoning me?*

★ *What am I curious about?*

★ *What kinds of texts should I gather to explore, and how do I find them?*

Choice recognizes that passion begins as awareness, which leads to curiosity. Children need opportunities to discover topics, issues, ideas, and authors, and then to explore and nourish curiosity. Choice also recognizes that readers may have varied reads in progress at any point in time, including texts they're reading with others and texts they're exploring alone. Children need reads that challenge the mind, as well as less challenging "beach reads." They need to learn to be thoughtful about which text they engage with on any given day, and why. And because they are reading in a community with others, they also need to be thinking about questions like these:

★   *Who else shares my interest, curiosity, or passion?*

★   *How can others open my eyes to new topics, ideas, and authors to explore?*

★   *How can we read, think and talk together?*

Children are also learning to make their way through more and more complex texts as they grow as readers. This complexity may present challenge. Learning to recognize and navigate challenge transitions children from knowing strategies to being strategic. We teach them to ask questions like these:

★   *What challenges does this text present for me?*

★   *How will I navigate these challenges?*

As children learn to engage with choice and complexity in reading workshop, they also begin to think strategically about community support. Becoming skilled at purposeful talk involves learning to balance time to contemplate alone with thinking and talking with others. Children may have assigned partners or be free to form their own collaborations. Either way, partners need to learn how to create a productive flow between *alone* and *together*. And they need to figure out when added voices might support them, and how to go about bringing them into a conversation.

In their work with partners, children draw from their developing understanding of talk, and take ownership of their efforts to think and talk together. Their conversations offer us an opportunity to listen and watch, confer, gauge the strength and transfer of our teaching, and make instructional decisions. In Chapter Seven we'll explore some framing questions that will help you as you observe and assess children's independent abilities with talk.

Finally, it's important to remember that the goal of the teaching cycle overviewed in this chapter—focus, facilitate, feedback—is to move children from support to independence. In his reflections on successful organizations, Simon Sinek wrote, "Average companies give their people something to work on. In contrast, the most innovative organizations give their people something to work towards" (2009, 99).

There's a parallel between the ways innovative companies engage people in pursuing a vision and the ways we should engage children in the pursuit of a literate life. It's easy to give children lots of stuff to work on, such as worksheets, reading activities, comprehension questions, centers, and exit slips. But do we help our children envision what it is that they're working toward? And do we design the learning opportunities that make pursuit of this vision a reality?

I would like to suggest that Jaylen and her classmates, whose conversation opened this chapter, know exactly what they're working toward. They're crafting purposefully literate lives. Lives where curiosity and passion fuel their reading, and their reading opens new visions of what's possible. Lives where engaging with ideas and with each other becomes foundational to constructing unique understandings. Reading workshop creates the space and time for these purposefully literate lives to develop.

Predictable Teaching for Unpredictable Talk

In the chapters that follow, we'll explore how to teach children talk behaviors that allow them to hear all voices (Chapter Four), grow ideas (Chapter Five), and negotiate meaning (Chapter Six). As we consider each behavior, you will see the same rhythmic cycle of teaching—focus, facilitate, feedback—suggested over and over again. As you've seen in this chapter, the cycle allows you to wrap your teaching around the messy, authentic work of children actually talking together.

You'll see that I offer examples of teaching language for focusing, facilitating, and offering feedback for each talk behavior along the way. If you notice that this language starts to sound a little repetitive, that means that the rhythm of the teaching cycle is becoming familiar to you, and that's a good thing! Too, some of the wording of facilitative moves may seem to overlap. The language will definitely have strong similarities, as the talk behaviors don't live in isolation from each other, and language that nudges at one will naturally support others.

My hope is that after reading these chapters, you will have internalized the cycle and can make it your own, even though it may take a while for it to feel natural in your teaching. Eventually, the repetition of focus, facilitate, and feedback will lead to a comfortable automaticity that allows you to meet the challenges of unpredictable talk with a fearless teaching spirit and sense of possibility.

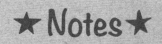

The best ideas emerge when very different perspectives meet.

—Frans Johansson

Four

Teaching Children to Hear All Voices

A Snapshot of Purposeful Talk

I am huddled on the carpet with a class of first graders who have been exploring the power of imagination. On this particular day, their inquiry has them delving into Jane Yolen's *What To Do With a Box* (2016). This delightful story, carried by Yolen's sparse rhyme, engages readers' imaginations along with the characters' as they transform a cardboard box from page to page. As the box morphs into a castle unlocked with a magic key—just in the nick of time to shelter characters and readers alike from a fierce dragon—Kylee's delight catches her teacher, Tess', attention:

> **Kylee:** AAAAH!
>
> **Tess:** [Laughing] Kylee?
>
> **Kylee:** The dinosaur's getting them!
>
> **Pedro:** No—a dragon! See! [Pointing to the dragon's nose]. The fire comes out!
>
> **Joshua:** It's a castle—they're pretending so it's safe. It's got magic—
>
> **Aiden:** [Shaking head] No—the key is magic!
>
> **Tess:** [Looking around circle, sees Lulu raising up on knees, head shaking vehemently] Lulu?

Lulu: It's the imagining—IT does the magic!

Gabriel: Yeah, they're imagining!

Yanaris: It's magical! They imagine and it's magical—on the other ones [pages], too.

Jamarie: Where?

Kylee: Hey, Markus giggled! He did—like this! [Imitates Markus' giggle]

Logan: Oh—it's because maybe he's got thinking!

Tess: What should we ask Markus?

Many voices: Markus, why did you giggle? . . . Do you have thinking? . . . Markus, what did you giggle for? . . .

This little bit of talk is spunky, joyful, and deceptively powerful. Kylee's squeals—and her delight in what she perceives to be a dinosaur—launches a meaning-making exploration. The children are leaning into the literal, trying to make sense of what they're seeing. Then, Lulu has a different theory about the imagining and the source of the magic than Joshua and Aiden. This sparks broader thinking in Yanaris' mind, shifting the meaning making to another level.

The conversation also offers insights into the children's use of purposeful talk. Eight out of the twenty-two children were involved in this snippet. The others were engaged alongside them, heads swiveling from the text to the speaker, and from each speaker to the next. Some were nodding or shaking, and there were several quizzical faces pondering both the dragon and castle and the notion of the magical qualities of imagination. Then Markus, a voice that had been outwardly silent to that point, giggled. Kylee noticed, Logan wondered about the potential, and with a nudge from Tess, a new voice was invited into the conversation.

Why Hearing All Voices Matters

Even in this brief excerpt of talk, the way children listen and build on each other's ideas shows that they value each other's thinking. The attention to that giggle, and the quick response to invite a new voice into the conversation because there might be thinking there, is clear evidence that they are developing strategies to draw from, or hear, all voices in a conversation.

At a literal level, hearing all voices can easily be misconstrued as a checklist-able goal. Brian spoke today—check! Heard from Emma—check! In reality, though, the *why* behind hearing all voices has far greater depth, situating it at the very heart of purposeful talk's constructive potential. In Chapter One, we explored David Kelley's assertion that thinking and talking with others helps us "get to a place that you just can't get to in one mind," suggesting the power of differing perspectives. Our classrooms are naturally and thankfully composed of a unique range of voices, each with different life experiences and different ways of viewing the world. As children think and talk together, this rich range of perspectives helps them to construct understandings that are bigger and bolder than they might construct on their own. This is the intent behind hearing all voices. We want children to experience the constructive potency of many voices, honor each, and learn the value of their own.

Hearing all voices does present challenges, however. Just like adults, children have different patterns of participation in talk. Some have no trouble adding their voice early and often, and we hear their thinking loud and clear, multiple times over, in every conversation. It may be that these children actually talk to think. Or it may be that they don't yet understand the value of—or have strategies for—drawing thinking from others.

Other children tend to wrestle with thoughts internally first. Although silent on the outside, there is often a raging conversation on the inside. As Robin Alexander notes, "those who are not speaking at a given time participate no less actively by listening, looking, reflecting, evaluating" (2008, 42). A smirk or furrowed brow, a glint in an eye, or a sly smile may hint at what's simmering in a child's mind. For these children, ideas may emerge slowly in turn and talks as they use their partners to help tease out their thinking. Or, their voices may enter a whole-group conversation over time as the collective thinking gradually helps them to strengthen their own.

> **At a literal level, hearing all voices can easily be misconstrued as a checklist-able goal. Brian spoke today—check! Heard from Emma—check! In reality, though, the why behind hearing all voices has far greater depth, situating it at the very heart of purposeful talk's constructive potential.**

Too, we know from our own experience that, when ideas resonate or touch close to home, we tend to chime in easily and passionately. But when ideas are unfamiliar or perplexing, we may hang back, wrestling with uncertainty. As I suggest this, I'm thinking of my own extended conversation with friends, propelled by a Marketplace Money radio series focused on the Eastern Congo. Over the span of a week, we listened to and talked about daily segments exploring the process of reconstructing an economy in an area rich with mineral wealth, yet still lagging in human development. Engaging in this conversation was daunting, as my friends were surprisingly well versed in the issues. Struggling to form questions, and hesitant to offer naïve opinions, I held back early on, hovering on the edge of the conversation as I listened and pieced together bits of information and insights. Although relatively silent on the outside, my mind was a swirl of puzzlement, questions, and tentative insights. Gradually, I waded in, becoming an increasingly vocal participant.

In this same way, each child's participation may vary from conversation to conversation based on a variety of factors, including the nature of the ideas being discussed. The takeaway here is that hearing all voices isn't as simple as instituting systematic turn-taking protocols. Although initiated with the best of intentions, these protocols may actually override an authentic, constructive flow of talk by emphasizing quantity of talk and equity in turn taking over meaning making. Structured turn taking tends to frustrate our "talk early, talk often" children, and creates undue stress for our shy or more contemplative children. Too, protocols tend to emphasize compliance through extrinsic control of talk over the development of an intrinsic value for a rich range of voices, the development of internally controlled strategies for adding one's voice productively, and attention to the flow of meaning.

It may be more useful—and more in keeping with the nature of real conversational process—to consider each child's pattern of participation over time as we implement processes for drawing in all voices. Becoming comfortable with the varied ways children's voices engage in an ebb and flow of meaning making, ranging from quiet contemplation and tentativeness to passionate loquaciousness, encourages us to provide variation in talk opportunities, strategies, and supports.

Teaching Talk Behaviors for Hearing All Voices

Teaching children the value of hearing all voices begins with building their awareness—awareness of the power of drawing thinking from others; awareness of different patterns of participation; and awareness of each child's own particular pattern or talk personality. Our "talk early, talk often" children, especially, need support to notice who's talking and who's not and to see the ways other voices affect their thinking. As children develop awareness of variations in participation, they also develop a keen understanding of why it matters, and will be more open to using the talk behaviors we offer them for hearing all voices.

Being Silent

Sometimes, inviting new voices into a conversation is as simple as not talking. Staying silent is not about being disinterested or disengaged. Rather, it's a deliberate move to open space for children to think, form tentative beginnings of ideas, and wrestle a bit with the uncertainty that might keep them from voicing their thinking out loud.

To be certain, even a few moments of silence can be uncomfortable at first. To **focus** children on the importance of silence, we might say, *If I pause a bit, it's to give you time to think, and to get your thinking out. You don't need to wait for me to ask a question—if you have a thought or question of your own, add it to the conversation.*

> **Sometimes, inviting new voices into a conversation is as simple as not talking.**

Then, at key points, as we **facilitate,** we might look up from the text with a *Wow!* or a *Hmmm. . . .* And, we hold back, trusting that children are truly thinking brilliant thoughts—or the beginnings of brilliant thoughts—and that this thinking will find its way out. Invitations such as, *Take a moment of thinking time*, invite silence. Or we may cock our head, raise an eyebrow, or look around the circle with anticipation, offering a nonverbal rendition of, *I can't wait to hear what you're thinking!*

This moment or two of silence gives us an opportunity to notice. We may notice facial expressions showing the spark of an idea or confusion. We notice whose voice finds its way into the conversation, and whose doesn't. Then, as the first bits of thinking emerge, we notice what aspects of the text children are tuning into, and what aspects may not have caught their attention.

Our **feedback** then needs to help children see how the moments of quiet thinking led to stronger talk, or helped them steer the conversation in a particular direction, or ask a pivotal question. *After we thought for a bit, Rolland realized something wasn't making sense to him. He didn't wait for me to ask a question. Instead, he asked a question. We went back into the text to reread, and it helped us all to make sense of things.*

Reading Facial Expressions

As children engage in meaning making, we know that silence on the outside doesn't necessarily equate to silence on the inside. To draw outwardly quiet thinkers into conversations, we attend closely to facial expressions and body language, and use these cues to draw children in. This is exactly what a kindergarten teacher, Susie, was doing as she read "Little Miss Muffet" with her children and they came to the phrase "eating her curds and whey." Surveying the children, Susie noticed Abdul, whose head was tilting to the side, his nose wrinkling in confusion. "I have to stop right there. Abdul's face went like this," Susie notes, making a confused face. "What were you wondering about, Abdul?"

> *As children engage in meaning making, we know that silence on the outside doesn't necessarily equate to silence on the inside.*

The kinders giggle and lean forward to survey Abdul's face as he smiles up at Susie. "Eating her curds and whey?" Susie poses. Abdul nods as she asks, "Do you have a question?" Abdul starts to speak, then slowly shakes his head. "You're not sure, are you?" Susie continues. "Why don't you see if your partner knows what curds and whey are? Ask them—say, 'What's curds and whey?'" The kinders, still full of giggles, all take up Susie's suggestion, turn to their partners, and choruses of "What's curds and whey?" quickly fill the room.

Susie, reading Abdul's face, recognized that he was thinking intently, and most likely had an as-of-yet unvoiced question raging in his head. She capitalized on his expression to invite his voice, but Abdul's thoughts were simply too jumbled at that point to articulate. So Susie articulated for him, and Abdul experienced the constructive power of a question conjured inside his mind, even though his words didn't quite make it out on their own.

Not only is reading facial expressions and body language an important aspect of thinking and talking with others, it's also a gentle way to acknowledge a quiet child's thinking and a natural opening to invite their voice. We may **focus** children on this possibility by saying things like, *We've been noticing how much stronger our thinking is when we hear from lots of voices. To help us do this, let's watch facial expressions, and notice when someone who's been thinking quietly inside their head is smiling, or frowning, or looking surprised. If you notice this, you can ask that person what they're thinking.*

To **facilitate**, we're on the lookout for those gestures and facial expressions that reveal yet-to-be-voiced thinking. Comments such as, *I'm noticing shaking/nodding heads . . .* , or *I'm seeing frowns/grins/ puzzled looks . . .* , help children recognize when they have thoughts to add, and serve as an invitation to do so. As children become accustomed to you reading and responding to their expressions, they will begin to do the same. Prompts such as, *Is anyone noticing the expression on Abdul's face? I wonder what he's thinking . . .* entice children to take the reins.

Feedback should help children understand how noticing a nonverbal cue helped the group to hear otherwise-quiet voices: *When Abdul had that look on his face, we paused to hear his thinking. We realized we were all wondering about curds and whey. Taking time to talk about it helped us to understand that Little Miss Muffet was having breakfast and that's why she didn't notice the spider and was so scared. So, noticing the look on someone's face and asking about their thinking helps us!*

Encouraging Tentative Thinking

As children talk to understand, their initial thoughts are often tentative in nature, marked by expressions such as, *I think . . .* or *Maybe . . .* We see this tentative, exploratory talk in the first graders' thinking and talking about Jane Yolen's *What To Do With a Box*. A dinosaur? A dragon? Is it the castle that's magic, or the key? Or is the power of imagination the real magic? Each of these tentative thoughts has the power to spark bigger thinking. Markus was either reveling in this tentative thinking, or he had his own possibilities brewing— hence, his giggle. To truly gather from a range of voices, we

> **As children talk to understand, their initial thoughts are often tentative in nature, marked by expressions such as, I think . . . or Maybe . . .**

need to create an environment that honors this tentativeness, as opposed to creating an expectation of fully fleshed-out (and grammatically correct) responses or answers.

When we **focus** children on the possibilities opened by tentative, exploratory thinking, we say things like, *We've been noticing the importance of getting our thinking out, even if it's still a bit uncertain. Little bits of thoughts spark thinking in other people, and that's important if we're going to grow ideas together. Today, notice if you have beginning thinking, and add it to our conversation so others can help to grow it.*

To **facilitate** and support children as they confidently voice tentativeness, the key is to actively invite beginning thinking: *Who has a thought? Is anyone wondering . . . ? Why might . . . ?* Tentative thinking not only encourages wondering and questions, but it also draws out elaborations or explorations that strengthen the current line of thought, or ideas that create doubt, causing all to rethink. Responding to tentative thinking can be as simple as showing we're intrigued by leaning in with a *Hmmm . . .*, confirming for children that they don't need fully formed ideas to engage.

Feedback should focus on the thinking that grew from tentativeness. It may sound like this: *Today, we talked a lot about what was in the heart of our characters. It started when DiAngelo said that something was happening between two of them, even though he wasn't sure exactly what it was yet. Adding that thinking mattered, because then Kyle realized he was feeling the same way. He said that he thought it was meanness, and that got us thinking closely about one of the character's words. Now we know more about the ways a character's words help us to understand. That's why it's important to add your thinking any time you're talking together, even if you're still a bit unsure.*

Honoring Questions

When wrestling with new thinking, children's first response may be puzzlement, which often emerges in the form of questions. Honoring these questions bolsters children's understanding that they don't need fully constructed ideas to add their voice to a conversation.

The children talking about *What To Do With a Box* were willing to voice their tentative thinking as they considered the origin of the magic they saw in the illustrations. Lulu linked the magic to the power of imagination, which piqued the interest of Gabriel and Yanaris. Surely there were a few questions forming as that thought settled in, and we want children to see that sharing their questions makes an important contribution to the constructive process.

> **When wrestling with new thinking, children's first response may be puzzlement, which often emerges in the form of questions.**

As we **focus** children on honoring questions, we remind them of the power of their own questions as they construct meaning: *As we think and talk together today, you may have questions bubbling up in your head. We know that these questions help us to dig in—so be sure to ask them out loud!*

Then, as we **facilitate**, a simple way to create space for children's questions is by pausing at critical points and asking, *What are you wondering?* or *What has you curious?* And, as challenging as it is, we need to resist the temptation to answer children's questions ourselves. Instead, we offer prompts such as, *Hmmm—what do you all think?* This helps children realize that their classmates' questions are theirs to tackle, and serves as an invitation for adding more voices.

To help children recognize the power of their own questions, we offer **feedback** that traces meaning making back to those questions: *Today, we explored the feelings between two characters using their thoughts and actions. Our thinking helped us to better understand each character. This work all started when Johana asked a question, and you all took it up and wrestled with it. When you notice you have questions, be sure to ask them!*

Using Turn and Talk Purposefully

The turn and talk plays a pivotal role in hearing all voices. But, too often, turn and talks are scheduled into conversations as a matter of protocol. To be more productive, turn and talks need to be used thoughtfully as a flexible support for the ongoing meaning making.

Complexity has a way of silencing even the most talkative groups. A turn and talk can be a strategic move when children are struggling. Time with a partner gives all children the opportunity to articulate confusion, ask questions, clarify, or retrace the thinking. This time for productive struggle also allows us to listen in on partner conversations, alert for footholds that might move the conversation forward when we reconvene.

We also need to be prepared for times when meaning making hits a combustive high and we seem to be hearing all voices all at once. A turn and talk allows for a productive harnessing of that energy as children satisfy their need to talk immediately.

Perhaps most importantly, a turn and talk supports more reticent voices. A few minutes with a trusted partner may help children build confidence to add a tentative thought to the whole-group conversation. Of course, when a quieter or more contemplative child engages in turn and talk, the more talkative partner may be the one who ends up sharing the pair's thinking with the whole group. Even if this is the case, the turn and talk has enabled the quieter child's perspective to become part of the collective thinking. This is the primary purpose behind hearing all voices, so it's critical that we're listening in on these partnerships and nudging this.

To **focus** children on using turn and talks more productively, we might say something like, *Today, we may use a turn and talk. If we do, remember this is an opportunity for you to share tentative thinking, ask questions, or have your partner help you think about ideas that seem confusing.*

As the whole group talks together, we watch for waning talk, points where the children all seem to need to talk at once, or points where a turn and talk might support the quieter voices. If we see this happen, we **facilitate** by inviting children to turn to their partners and take a few minutes to think and talk together. As we listen, we may check in on our quieter children, our "talk early, talk often" children, and partnerships that seem to be building provocative thinking. Then, to bring this thinking and these voices into the larger conversation, we might say to the partners, *That's an interesting thought. Let's bring the group back together and see what the others think.* The amount of support we offer here will depend on the specific children. If we're drawing out a more reticent voice, we may orchestrate partner support, or lean in ourselves.

When this happens, the **feedback** should acknowledge the quiet child as the origin of, or a voice in, the thinking that was shared: *During our turn and talk, Benji asked a question that really made Tatianna think. They had a tentative idea that Tatianna shared with the group. Benji's question, and his thinking with Tatianna, helped us to grow that new idea.* This feedback helps all to understand the potential of the turn and talk, and has the added benefit of helping quieter children like Benji understand the power of their voice.

Inviting Others into the Conversation

As children begin to understand the value of many voices, we need to nudge them to actually invite more voices into the conversation. The goal is to help children—talkative ones especially—attend to the range of voices in a conversation because they're learning to value others' thinking—not because of rules or protocols that aim to limit their airtime.

We might **focus** this work in this way: *We've been noticing that our quiet thinkers sometimes have ideas we haven't talked about. If you notice we haven't heard someone's thinking yet, you might ask them if they're ready to add it.* We can also frame the focus to specifically highlight *why* it's helpful to invite new thinking into a conversation. *Today, pay attention to how your thinking is growing or shifting. If you realize your thinking* isn't *growing or shifting, invite new voices into the conversation.*

Facilitation is then angled toward our talkative children, basically inviting them to invite others: *Naomi, it looks like Kenny has thinking. Why don't you ask him about it?* Or, when an expected voice emerges again, we might pause and say, *Hmmm, I wonder how that thought is settling with everyone. Try inviting a few people into the conversation to find out!*

Finally, **feedback** should help children reflect on the degree to which thoughts from others helped their thinking to grow. We might notice and name like this: *Naomi, when you asked Hallie what she thought about your idea, she actually disagreed. Her reason gave us all new thinking. That's exactly why it's such a good move to invite new voices into the conversation!*

You may find it helpful to include private focus and feedback time for more persistent "talk early, talk often" children, too. In *Talking About Text*, I share how I helped Monique, a former student, develop an awareness of her own talkative nature (2008, 103–105). It was a long journey, but eventually Monique's reflective process morphed into daily musings about the ways her thinking grew and shifted because of others' ideas. She gradually came to realize that, if her thinking didn't grow or shift, she needed to up her listening effort.

Writing Your Way into the Conversation

In our classrooms, we often create charts as we're talking with children to track the thinking as it unfolds, making the ongoing meaning-making process visible. We can also invite children to jot thoughts or questions on sticky notes and add them to our charts on their own as they continue to grow their ideas. Adding thinking with sticky notes may happen as children revisit the text, gain insights from different texts, or simply as they continue thinking and talking about the ideas. Sticky notes are also helpful tools for quieter children, or those who need more time to formulate thinking, to add their voice to the conversation.

To encourage children to use this option, we **focus** children on this option at the *end* of a conversation: *As you think more about this, if you have a new idea, question, or wondering, write it on a sticky note and add it to our chart! I'll leave the sticky notes right here. Be sure to add your name so others can talk with you about your thinking.* We may even nudge by adding a sticky note of our own at some point in the day, placing it where—and when—little eyes will be sure to notice!

When children do add thinking to a chart, we survey the possibilities and choose one or two promising lines of thinking to engage the class on subsequent days. For example, a first-grade class had been reading Jim Arnosky's *Raccoons and Ripe Corn* (1991), a delightful tale of a raccoon family stealing from a cornfield under the cover of darkness to feast. During the whole-group conversation, Cali, who tends toward the more contemplative end of the participation spectrum, had engaged in turn and talks, and intently followed the conversation, but we had not heard her voice in the whole group. Later that day, a pink sticky note appeared on the chart. This sticky note held a single question, and it was signed by none other than Cali. It read, "Do the pepl no?"

The next day, as we revisited the text, I reminded the children that the notes are a way to add new thinking to a conversation, and then I brought Cali's thinking to the group. Notice my **facilitation** moves:

> **Maria:** [Reading Cali's sticky note] Cali asked, "Do the people know?" Cali, what people are you wondering about?
>
> **Cali:** At the farm.
>
> **Nicola:** It has a farm?

Maria: [Turns to the page showing the barn, farmhouse, and corn field]

Jamie: And a house!

Ben: Maybe the farmer goes there.

Maria: So, what Cali is asking is, do the people—the farmer—do they know that the raccoons are eating their corn?

James: [Hands on his head] Eeeiii! They did it at night! He's [the farmer] gonna be mad!

"Eeeiii!" Is exactly right. We had talked about the raccoons and their habits and motives, but had not considered the raccoons' antics through the perspectives of the farmer.

In offering **feedback,** be sure to highlight the ways the note—and the student's voice—lifted the meaning making, and encourage children to continue to use writing to record their ideas. *We're fortunate that Cali captured her thinking on a sticky note yesterday. If she hadn't, we might have never even thought about the farmer and what he was thinking. Thank you, Cali! Don't forget to use these notes any time you have new thoughts to add.*

Facilitative Language Shifts

Growing children's understanding of hearing all voices shifts the focus from compliance and turn taking to helping children understand the power of their own voices, and the importance of drawing in others. The process of **focus, facilitate,** and **feedback** teaches children to actively seek a range of voices and perspectives in their conversations. We first pose questions such as, *Who haven't we heard from?* and *Who else could you talk to?,* but slowly our children come to own these language moves, developing habits for thinking and talking together purposefully and independently.

The chart in Figure 4.1 highlights some simple language shifts discussed in this chapter to help as we facilitate conversations. These subtle shifts send important messages about whose voices are valued, and they also position children to take more and more responsibility for inviting others into their talk (see the far-right column).

Facilitative Language Shifts For Hearing All Voices

Instead of saying . . .	Try saying this . . .
I think . . . *I noticed . . .* *I want to know . . . Who can tell me . . .?*	*[silence]* *Hmmm . . .*
___, *it's your turn now.*	*I'm noticing shaking/nodding heads . . . what are you thinking?* *I'm seeing frowns/grins/puzzled looks . . . what are you thinking?*
Who knows how/why/when . . .?	*Who has a thought?* *Is anyone wondering . . . ?* *Why/how might . . . ?* *Hmmmm . . .*
My question is . . . *Now, my next question is . . .*	*What has you curious?* *What are you wondering?* *Your thinking has me wondering . . .*
This one's hard. Let me explain . . .	*Take a few minutes to think and talk this through with your partner.*
___, *it's your turn now.* *I'm sorry* ___, *you've already spoken three times.*	*I'm curious about how a new voice might shift our thinking. Does anyone want to add in a question, tentative wondering, or idea?* *Whose ideas have changed your thinking? Let's invite more of their thinking.*
OK, we've decided that this book is about . . .	*As you keep thinking about this, be sure to add your new ideas or questions to our chart. Then, we can revisit our thinking to grow it further.*

What's the difference?	Transferring facilitation
Shifts responsibility for the thinking and talking from the teacher to the children. Offers children space to think a bit, and sets the tone of the talk itself.	*Are you noticing what happens when we take a minute just to think?*
Shifts from cold-calling on children with an emphasis on turn taking, to noticing and responding to nonverbal signs of thinking. Invitation is responsive to children's internal process, drawing them into the conversation in gentle ways.	*Are you noticing shaking/nodding heads? Are you wondering what they're thinking? How might you ask . . . ?* *Look around the circle—are you seeing frowns/grins/puzzled looks? Are you wondering what they're thinking? How might you ask . . . ?*
Shifts from a search for answers to an invitation for tentative thinking, which opens the conversation to a greater range of ideas and voices.	*Who might have a thought? How might you ask . . . ?* *Are you curious about the wondering in people's heads? How might you ask . . . ?*
Shifts from the teacher as the asker of predetermined questions to sincere, responsive questions from both teacher and students. Frames curiosity and wonder as critical parts of the construction of meaning.	*Are you curious about the wondering in people's heads? How might you ask . . . ?* *What does their thinking get you wondering about? How might you ask . . . ?*
Offers partner support for challenging ideas. Shows a belief in children's own strategic process to take on and talk through challenging ideas.	*Remember, if you need partner talk time to talk things through, let us know.*
Shifts from teacher control of turn taking or an expectation of quiet voices finding their own way into a conversation to a process that supports and encourages them to add their voices. Shifts from extrinsic control of turn taking for our "talk early, talk often" children to helping them learn the potential of other voices and strategies needed for inviting them. Focuses children on the evolution of their thinking, emphasizing comprehension as an ongoing process.	*Is there anyone you need to invite into the conversation?* *Hmmm . . . I wonder how that thought is settling with everyone. Try inviting a few people into the conversation to find out!* *It looks like ___ has some thinking. How might you ask him/her about it?*
Shifts from comprehension as a finite process with a clear ending, to a process of comprehending that's ongoing. Offers more reticent children a tool for adding their thinking to the conversation.	*How might you keep these ideas growing?*

A full-size version of this table can be downloaded from http://hein.pub/biggerideas (click on Companion Resources).

The most important parts
of any conversation
are those that
neither party
could have imagined
before starting.

—William Isaacs

Five

Teaching Children to Grow Ideas

A Snapshot of Purposeful Talk

It's a damp mid-winter Monday morning, and I'm grateful my day is beginning with an always-lively first-grade class. I walk through the door and, true to form, find Devin gleefully bobbing up and down on the carpet, children circled around him as his arms wave and curl through the air. "It goes like that!" he exclaims to his classmates' giggles and exclamations. "And it smashed really big and pushed me!" He laughs as he rolls himself backward.

Puzzled, I look to the children's teacher, Kurt, who flips the book they're reading to the cover for me . . . and then it all makes sense. The children were—forgive the pun—wading into Suzy Lee's *Wave* (2008). This wordless picture book lures readers into the delightful intersection of a beach, a curious girl, and some playful waves. Devin, it seems, was adding his own encounter with waves to the conversation. Still holding center court, he rolls himself upright and continues, "I got scared—just like her." This thought immediately sparks debate among the group.

Emma: She's not scared!

Many voices: Yeah, she is . . . Not anymore . . . No, 'cuz it's fun now . . .

Kurt: Quick—talk to your partner. What are you thinking about her—and why?

The children quickly turn, and the noise level rises as pairs and trios work to make sense of the girl's emotions. Some are imitating her facial expression, and others, motivated by Devin, are drawing from their own experiences. Kurt leans in to listen and nudge, then pulls the class back together.

Kurt: I heard a few of you talking about the girl being scared at first, but now you're not sure. What's that about?

Lyla: Maybe she got braver.

Benji: But—how can she?

Miguel: [Bouncing up on his knees] Oh yeah—like me and Danny— um—um—when we ride skateboards—huh? [Looking to Danny for confirmation]

Danny: We try tricks—it's kinda scary!

Miguel: He tried one—a trick. He tried and—um—he didn't. But he kept doing it, and he kinda kicked up. Then he did like this [doing a kneeling rendition of an end zone dance].

Many voices: [Laughing]

Kurt: OK—how does that help you to think about the girl in the story?

Miguel: Um—she's um—maybe like Danny. It's scary, but you—

Kendra: Oh—like you just do it a little bit.

Miguel: Yeah, yeah—um—a little bit. And you get brave.

Missy: If you try, you can get braver.

Kurt: OK—let's look back through the pictures and see if we notice her getting braver. When we started, I told you this author tells her story without words, and—

Chase: [Interrupting] It's OK. We're growing words for her!

And with that, I half expected Kurt to go into his own rendition of an end zone dance. Such a change from the beginning of the year, when these same children had to be coaxed into talking at all. Now, within a few minutes' time, the children's talk has carried them from working to understand a little girl's interaction with a wave to the beginnings of some deeper explorations of fear, perseverance, and change. They're doing so much more than growing words—they're actually growing ideas.

As notable as the children's work is, it's also worth noting what Kurt is doing—or perhaps more importantly, what he's *not* doing. Specifically, he did not affirm *scared* or *brave* as correct emotions for the girl, or label the girl permanently with either trait. And, although the children are nudging toward big ideas, he didn't ask them to name the main idea or theme of the story. Kurt knows that there may still be varied interpretations of the girl's emotions, as well as multiple big ideas swirling in the space between the pages and these children's worlds. He also knows they'll revisit the text, think, and talk more, and he trusts that their understanding will continue to evolve. Yes, this is the perfect start to a midwinter Monday morning!

Why Growing Ideas Matters

When wrestling with complex ideas, children's thinking often emerges tentatively, offering glimmers of possibility. We hear this in Lyla's thought: "Maybe she got braver." But there's work to be done with these possibilities if they're to become truly meaningful. Prompts such as *What are you thinking?* or *Is anyone wondering about . . .* open the conversation up for children to pursue these tentative beginnings, their exploratory talk becoming the seeds for bigger, bolder ideas.

> **When wrestling with complex ideas, children's thinking often emerges tentatively, offering glimmers of possibility.**

However, if children jump from tentative thought to tentative thought without lingering and constructing, these seeds of possibilities evaporate into the air, unexplored. To shift this, children need to learn to pause, take in tentative beginnings, and talk them into something bigger. Teaching children to grow ideas shifts their talk from telling to constructing as they engage in a range of talk behaviors that support three main goals. To grow ideas, children must learn how to

★ say something meaningful

★ listen with intent

★ keep lines of thinking alive.

Each of these goals presents its own challenges, of course, and in the sections that follow, we'll consider the challenges first before we move into the specific talk behaviors that support each goal. As you read through, just keep in mind that even though it's helpful to consider the distinct goals for these different talk behaviors, the intent is that they all serve the larger goal of helping children use talk to grow big, bold ideas.

Teaching Talk Behaviors for Growing Ideas: Say Something Meaningful

The goal of teaching children to say something meaningful is to help them become aware of and articulate the connection between their thinking and the ongoing conversation. We also want children to learn to differentiate between thoughts that have the potential to grow thinking, and those random thoughts that can pop into heads and distract.

In truth, it's very normal for totally random thoughts—fascinating, odd, and often-hilarious word associations or connections—to pop into children's heads as they think and talk with others. In casual, social contexts, this mental meandering can be quite enjoyable. But when we're thinking and talking purposefully, continuously giving in to these random thoughts challenges constructive intent. The tricky thing is, it can be challenging to figure out whether a child's thought connects, or not.

For example, I was once reading Peter Hansard's *A Field Full of Horses* (2001) with a group of second graders. The children and I were thinking and talking about Hansard's obvious admiration for horses, and the ways his word choice revealed this. It was all going so well . . . until we came to a bold illustration of a mare with flies swarming all around her head. I had scarcely finished reading the page aloud—". . . and then she gives a sudden shiver to keep the flies away"—when Bobby exploded into the conversation. "Oh no!" he exclaimed. "That doesn't work! I try that—with my hands [waving his hands as if shooing away flies]—but the flies don't go. I even swallowed one!"

I'm sure you know exactly what happened from there . . .

Gwen: Ewwww!

Troy: Once, I swallowed a fly! Ants, too! They got on my—

Brandon: Oh man—my little sister once, she ate a—a—what do you call it? The rolly ones?

Troy: —on my hot dog.

Many voices: Oh—oh me, too . . . I ate a . . . Oh gross! . . . a beetle bug . . . and it flew right in . . . ewww . . . once, my dad ate . . .

Yup—you guessed it. The majesty of horses was completely lost to the horrors of accidental entomophagy. It was a tough recovery. But Bobby wasn't just "being bad" or trying to be silly. Rather, his mind was naturally doing what all our minds do. He may have realized a connection between his funny story and the horse in the text. His annoyance with flies does have the potential to help build empathy for the mare. Or, the illustration may have triggered this memory randomly, with no real connection in his mind. Children like Bobby need to learn to consider both options, make a connection visible if there is one, or let the idea go—at least temporarily—if there isn't.

As we support children in the work of saying something meaningful, it's important to take an inquiry stance. We don't want to move too quickly and judge a child's thought without giving it—and the child—a chance. Doing this undermines constructive intent and tentative beginnings, as well as the value for ideas and perspectives we're working so hard to build. When a child offers what seems to be a random thought, we need to move gently to figure out if the thought is a bit of divergent brilliance that just needs to be dug into a little, or the result of a mind that's wandering. It takes time, but with thoughtful discussion and teaching, even our youngest learners can learn to do the work of connecting divergent thoughts for others, or recognizing a random thought and parking it for later.

> **As we support children in the work of saying something meaningful, it's important to take an inquiry stance.**

Becoming Aware of Random Thoughts

A good place to begin this work is to simply help children become aware that some of the thoughts that pop into our heads strengthen a conversation, while others distract us from that conversation. As I talk with children about random, disconnected thoughts, I frame having them as being a very human thing, emphasizing that it's just what our brains do sometimes. Again, this is critical, as we don't want to inadvertently create a fear of voicing thinking.

We can help children **focus** on this talk behavior by alerting them to the potential for this to happen: *We've been noticing that sometimes thinking pops into our heads that doesn't quite fit with the big ideas we're exploring. It happens to everybody. If we say the thinking out loud, it can distract us from our conversation. Let's pay attention to that today, and think about what we can do if that happens.* We might also suggest strategies such as "parking a thought" (introduced in my book *Comprehension Through Conversation*): *One thing we can try is parking the thinking for later. That means settling the thought on the side of your brain, so that you can talk about it another time.*

Facilitation then supports children's efforts. When Bobby launched into his bug-eating escapades, what I might have said is, *Bobby, I wonder how that experience helps you understand the horses?* What I say next depends on his response. If it is truly a random thought, and Bobby doesn't think it has anything to do with the horses, I might say, *Oh, I think I know what your brain just did! You saw the horse trying to shoo flies, and it reminded you of a funny time with your dad. I wonder whether that funny story is going to help us as we talk about the ways Peter Hansard connects with horses, or if this is something you might park for later? What do you think?* Inviting Bobby into the process honors his ability to reflect on his thoughts and suggests his disconnected thought might be worthy of later exploration, as opposed to simply labeling it as "wrong."

When we're aware that children have made thoughtful decisions about notions that pop into their heads, we can offer **feedback** that names what they've done and why doing it mattered. What I might have said to Bobby and his bug-eating pals if he realized his story didn't connect is, *Today, Bobby started to add a funny story to our conversation. But then he realized it was going to pull us away from thinking about Peter Hansard and the way he writes about horses. So, he decided to hold on to that funny story to enjoy later, and we focused back on our thinking.* Of course, it's very possible you won't realize children have held on to random thoughts, so if teaching this behavior is your focus, you might spend a few moments after a whole-class conversation asking children about the random thoughts they kept to themselves, and see what you can learn from their decisions.

Connecting Thoughts

I wonder whether that funny story is going to help us as we talk about the ways Peter Hansard connects with horses. . . . The tentative *I wonder* in this facilitation is worth a second look. As I noted earlier, there is always the possibility that a seemingly random thought is actually a line of divergent brilliance simply in need of an explanation. Because this potential exists, we need to teach children how to make the connection between their private thoughts and the ongoing meaning making clear to others.

> **There is always the possibility that a seemingly random thought is actually a line of divergent brilliance simply in need of an explanation.**

To **focus** children on this behavior, we teach them to look for signs—usually nonverbal cues—that show that a connection is *not* clear to others. We might say something like, *Sometimes when you add thoughts to a conversation, you might notice that some of your class-mates have a confused look on their faces, or say things like "Huh?" If that happens, it means you need to help them understand how your thought connects to the ideas we're talking about. Let's watch for that today.*

As we **facilitate**, we pay attention to nonverbal cues and watch for signs that a connection isn't clear, but we don't necessarily jump right in. Sometimes, a little space helps connections become clear, and if it doesn't, then we can nudge a little. As I listened to the first graders talking about *Wave*, I wasn't sure how Miguel and Danny's skateboarding escapades connected to their conversation about the book. But Kurt wisely let the thinking flow for a bit, then asked a critical question: *How does that help you to think about the girl in the story?* This simple question nudged Miguel to link his and Danny's experiences and emotions to his under-standing of the character, which led to a deepening understanding for all.

Feedback should highlight the way a child has made a connection clear to others. In the first-grade classroom where they were reading *Wave*, for example, Kurt might have said something like, *Miguel and Danny added thinking about skateboarding to our conversation today. I was confused at first, but then Manuel explained how thinking about Danny trying flips helped him to make sense of the girl in our book. His explanation helped us all to dig back into the illustrations and think more about the character.* Then, he could build for transfer by saying, *When you add a thought to a conversation, you might need to explain how it connects to and helps to grow the thinking.*

Teaching Talk Behaviors for Growing Ideas: Listen with Intent

> *If children are to use talk to construct, they must listen with a willingness to have their thinking changed, and value the potential of others to change it.*

In Chapter One, we explored the constructive beauty of eloquent listening, which Senator Howard Baker considered to be the essence of leadership. William Isaacs, author of *Dialogue: The Art of Thinking Together*, agrees, proposing that, "The heart of dialogue is a simple but profound capacity to listen." This depth of listening, what I refer to as *listening with intent*, is both purposeful and respectful (1999, 83). If children are to use talk to construct, they must listen with a willingness to have their thinking changed, and value the potential of others to change it. Listening with intent means learning to balance opportunities to add your thinking to a conversation with opportunities to take in others' words, intently engage with their minds, and work to understand.

> *Listening with intent means learning to balance opportunities to add your thinking to a conversation with opportunities to take in others' words, intently engage with their minds, and work to understand.*

This balance is not always easy to find. The Greek philosopher Epictetus is quoted as saying, "Nature gave us one tongue and two ears so we could hear twice as much as we speak." Yet sometimes, those two ears don't seem to be quite enough. We mean to listen, we begin to listen, but then something someone says triggers a thought that reminds us of something we need to do, or an e-mail we need to send, or gets us wondering about something completely disconnected, and next thing you know, our mind is meandering. This is called being human.

Our children are no less human. Annah shares a brilliant idea, and you ask, "Did everyone listen to Annah's idea?" All heads nod yes, so you ask, "What do you think about it?" You turn to one child, and then another, and another . . . and it quickly becomes clear that no one really listened to Annah's thinking.

So, what gets in their way? One possibility is that children, like us, are simply distracted by their own thoughts. They're aware of someone talking, but the words float by as they puzzle through and rehearse their own thinking, anticipating (or plotting to create) an opening in the conversation so they can talk. Some may be following random thoughts down a rabbit hole. Others may begin reacting to a classmate's thinking before he or she fully articulates his idea. They take in just enough of the thought to get a sense of direction, and then run with it—or over it.

Part of the struggle may also be that we send unintended messages about listening. Too often, we use the ability to retell as our gauge for listening. Protocols such as, "Tell what your partner said" actually set the listening bar quite low. It's possible to comply without any intent to draw from your partner's thinking—indeed, without actually understanding his or her thinking.

And, all too often, we focus on the etiquette of listening rather than the actual in-the-head work of listening. We ask children to sit up straight, face the speaker, and make eye contact. These behaviors may support listening to a degree. However, as a world-class daydreamer, I'm all too aware of my own ability to lean in and make eye contact—and still be a million miles away in my head. Listening with intent is more than just making eye contact and holding on to someone's words long enough to repeat them. We need to engage our minds and hearts in coordination with our ears, actively turning others' words into meaningful thought.

As adults, we have strategies to deal with our all-too-human lapses in listening. They range from the less productive, such as nodding and pretending we're following along, to far more desirable moves, such as recognizing our momentary distraction and asking for thoughts to be repeated. We need to help children develop awareness of their own listening, teach them productive strategies to get back into the conversation if listening lapses, and strategies for maintaining that listening.

Becoming Aware of Listening

In *Listen Hear! 25 Effective Listening Comprehension Strategies*, Michael Opitz differentiates passive, surface level hearing from truly listening by suggesting, "Hearing is a sound; listening is a thought" (2004, 2). Building awareness is the first step in helping children differentiate between hearing and really listening.

We can **focus** children on awareness by reminding them of the *why* behind listening with intent and the importance of taking thinking in from others. *Today, as we're talking, remember that when you're really listening, you're having thoughts about what someone is saying.*

Figure 5.1 Thinking About the Difference Between Hearing and Listening

Visuals, such as the chart pictured in Figure 5.1, can help children, especially our youngest learners, understand the somewhat abstract difference between hearing and listening. Notice the children's sticky note additions, layered on as they began differentiating between hearing as background sound, like a lawnmower outside the classroom, as opposed to the thinking and sense of a full brain that develops when they're really listening.

To **facilitate** listening awareness productively, it's important to treat wobbles in listening as simply being human, as opposed to "being bad" or having deficits as a learner. I try to frame my responses so I show children I'm human, too, by saying things like, *Oh—that happens to me, too! I mean to listen, but my own thinking just gets in the way.* Then, I offer a strategy. *Here's what I do—I look at the person who was talking and say, will you please repeat that?* And then—this is crucial—I have the child give it a go. Our youngest learners tend to love doing this and will often take it to extremes before the behavior becomes a norm. Older children are apt to be a bit hesitant, fearing embarrassment, or not really believing that they aren't "in trouble." But if we're consistent in addressing this as being human, and consistent in welcoming children's efforts to take responsibility, they'll begin speaking up when they realize their listening has dropped off.

Feedback for listening with intent should focus on the moves children made to adjust for a momentary lapse in listening, and the difference it made: *When Mattie realized she didn't completely focus on Jared's idea, she leaned over and asked him to repeat it. This was really important; because then Jared's thought made Mattie ask a question, and then that question made us all rethink what was really happening. So, noticing what's happening with your own listening, and taking action when you realize someone's words slid by you, is something we should do in all conversations!*

Listening with a Readiness Stance

Thinking of this phase of the work takes me back to the joy of tennis lessons. I hear my coach bellowing over and over, "readiness position!" Not knowing what direction the incoming shot might take, my knees were bent and my weight was shifting side-to-side, enabling alertness and quick feet, ready to move. In this same way, we want children in a "readiness stance" when they're listening. Ears, mind, and heart need to be alert, prepared to take in the thinking and move with it, responding, questioning, and feeling.

To **focus** children on their listening readiness, we can remind them of how quickly thoughts slide past us if we're not ready. We might say, *As we talk today, we're going to work on being ready to listen, and noticing what happens to our thinking when we do.*

Facilitating a readiness stance often includes suggestions of what to be ready for, such as listening for the logic behind a thought. When a child is about to speak, we can quickly nudge listeners by saying something like, *Amika has an idea. Let's listen closely to make sure we understand her thinking.* Or, we might cue children to listen for ideas they can use as springboards: *Listen to Diego's thinking and notice if it makes you wonder anything.* We might prepare children to listen for the emotion behind a response, saying, *Listen closely and watch Callie's face to see how she's feeling about this.* And, if we sense disagreement, we might ask children to listen for a new way of seeing an idea: *Let's listen to see if Chrystal has a different way of thinking about this.*

Then, **feedback** needs to key in on the ways children's listening led to deeper meaning: *Amika was listening for the ways Carter's thinking made her wonder. She added her wonder to the conversation, and that led us to an important question.*

The intent here is not to lock children into a singular way of listening and responding. I'm not suggesting weeks of instruction focusing in on just listening for difference, for example. Rather, the intent is to build an auditory and cognitive equivalence of a readiness stance.

Reflecting as Relistening

Reflection can be a powerful tool for deepening listening. When we reflect, we continue to engage in the meaning-making process in a multitude of ways, discovering more possibility and greater depth in others' words. In essence, when we reflect, we relisten. Encouraging this is actually part of teaching children to extend conversations over time, returning to ideas with new insights and questions.

When we **focus** on the power of reflection to help us hear more and develop reflective habits, we might start by sharing our own reflective practice. For example, we might open a conversation by revisiting the previous day's talk, showing children how ideas have lingered in our thinking. *Tara, I was thinking more about the thoughts you added to our conversation yesterday. We were talking about the things our characters were doing and why, and you said maybe they're tired. Yesterday, I thought you meant tired, like sleepy. But as I listened to you again in my mind, I started to think you mean more like just so tired of having to deal with everything. That new idea changed my thoughts on the characters. Was anyone else listening to Tara's thinking again inside their head? What are you thinking now?*

Gradually, we want to invite children to take the lead in drawing from reflection. We **facilitate** this by simply asking, *Who thought more about our ideas last night? Did anyone's words linger with you? Is there a thought or idea that you can't let go of?* Or we might frame it even more specifically as, *Did you have any "ahas!" or new questions?*

Our **feedback** then, notices and names the power of that reflection. *Jenny was thinking more about what Bradley said yesterday. She heard his words inside her head, and really listened and thought more about them. Now she understands his thinking better, and she asked a great question because of it. Her question launched more thinking and talking, and now we all understand more. Any time you think more about someone's idea, be sure to add that new thinking!*

Teaching Talk Behaviors for Growing Ideas: Keep Lines of Thinking Alive

When we teach children to say something meaningful and listen with intent, we've made a great start toward building purposeful talk, but there's more work to do. Once the tentative thoughts start bubbling up, we want to avoid going around the circle for rounds of "I think . . ." that go poof into the air. Instead, we need to teach children how to push the pause button on a thought, engage in uptake with each other, and talk tentative beginnings into lines of thinking. Then, children need support in learning to hold on to these lines of thinking as they read more, think more, and talk more—continually growing them into bigger, bolder possibilities.

> ❝ We need to teach children how to push the pause button on a thought, engage in uptake with each other, and talk tentative beginnings into lines of thinking. ❞

Developing the ability to hold their own thought while focusing fully on and growing someone else's thinking takes time. Children's natural inclination is to rush to tell their thinking. It may be that they're fully captivated by their idea, and out of sheer exuberance, out it comes. Or they may be concerned about forgetting their thinking—and rightly so. We ask a child to hold his thinking while we focus on a different tentative thought and build it, but when we cycle back to that child, he can't remember. This, of course, is frustrating. If thinking is forgotten, we can sometimes help by backing up to the page or comment that prompted the thinking. If that doesn't work, we lessen the frustration a bit by saying, *Oh, that happens to me, too, sometimes. Let's read and talk a bit more, and see if your idea comes back.*

> ❝ Our goal after all is to help children slow down and think deeply—to engage in uptake—and develop openness toward each other's thinking, a willingness to shift their own thinking, and an awareness of the power in the process. ❞

Although the process of learning how to hold a thought and focus on others' thinking can be challenging, especially when we engage with twenty or more voices in a conversation, it is important enough that we shouldn't let a few forgotten thoughts deter us from progressing with this work. Our goal after all is to help children slow down and think deeply—to engage in uptake—and develop openness toward each other's thinking, a willingness to shift their own thinking, and an awareness of the power in the process.

Clarifying

It goes without saying that children can't grow thinking they don't understand. Yet too often, children either don't recognize their confusion, or they are passive and simply shrug it off. To **focus** children on the need for clarity, we ask them to be aware of thoughts or ideas that confuse them and then take an active stance: *Today, as we're thinking and talking together, if someone's idea isn't clear, be sure to ask that person to explain their thinking.*

As tentative thoughts are voiced, we **facilitate** by acknowledging and normalizing confusion, and teaching the specific kinds of questions that draw out explanation. This begins with looking for scrunchy faces and puzzled glances and listening for cries of "What?" and "Huh?" Then, when we see or hear them, we say something like, *Ah, it sounds like we have some confusion.*

Next, we teach children how to act on their uncertainty in ways that lead to clarity. We might scaffold the clarification, asking *Kamal, do you mean . . .* or *Letti, I think you're saying _____. Am I understanding you?* Or even something as simple as *Can you explain that a bit?*

Eventually, we turn the responsibility for asking for clarification over to children, so we say things like *Joey, I see the look on your face. Do you need Hallie to say more about her thinking?* Or we invite the child to ask: *Terrance, it sounds as if that didn't make sense to you. Why don't you ask Bryan to say more?* When children are asked to clarify a thought, it generally prompts them to rework the thought in their own mind, which also strengthens their thinking. They can then articulate the thought again, working to reword it with added clarity, or bolster it with added details.

Feedback for clarifying includes both recognizing confusion and taking an active stance: *Charlie realized he didn't understand Maya's thought, so he asked her to explain. As Maya said more about her thinking, Ella had an "aha!" moment that helped us understand the stance our author was taking. Noticing if you're confused and asking someone to explain, is always powerful.*

Lingering with a Thought

Once thinking is voiced and clarified if needed, we sometimes want to encourage a moment of lingering with the thought, mulling it over. We might **focus** children on the need to do this by saying, *Once someone adds their thinking, let's work on pausing for a moment to really think about it, and notice how it settles with our own thinking.*

To **facilitate**, questions such as *What does Ari's idea have you thinking?* encourage children to pause. Nudging with added questions such as *How does this idea lie next to your own thinking?* encourages even deeper consideration.

As children begin to linger with thoughts, we want to notice and name what they're doing and offer **feedback** on the ways slowing down supports their listening and thinking. *When Rachel added her thinking, we were all quiet for just a moment. I could tell you were really thinking about her idea. Then, Teri started to talk more about it. Taking that moment to really think about Rachel's idea helped Teri to grow it. Remember to slow down and take time to think as you talk with others throughout the day.*

Agreeing and Disagreeing

Agreeing and disagreeing are both ways of pushing and pulling with thinking that can deepen and broaden understanding. Protocols that rely on hand signals may offer a quick and orderly way of gaging agreement or disagreement, but they don't do much to push meaning making. Agreement needs to be voiced, along with any added reasoning. When we agree with a thought, we have the potential to bolster the logic behind the thinking or cite added rationale, all in service of deepening the thinking. This reasoning may be drawn from the text, other texts, or children's understanding of their world.

When we disagree, we put forward a contradictory rational, a different perspective, or a new way of seeing that broadens the thinking. Disagreement with a thought may come immediately, or it may slowly build. We watch for the shaking heads, the scrunched faces, the hands thrown up in despair. We listen for exclamations such as *No!* and *But . . . .* However it bubbles to the surface, disagreement needs to be voiced, again with reasoning.

To **focus** children on adding more to a conversation when they agree, we remind them that when someone says something they were going to say, or something that makes sense, they can strengthen the thought by adding more. *When you agree with someone, adding the reasons* why *you agree makes that thought stronger.* The same holds true for disagreement. *When you disagree with a thought, it might mean you have an important perspective we need to consider. Be sure to add your thinking!*

As we **facilitate**, we watch for signs of agreement in a conversation, like nodding heads and comments such as *Yeah!* or *That's what I think!* We also look for the child whose hand flops down in dejection because she thinks someone said her answer. *That's great!* we say, and ask, *Why are you thinking the same way?* We might also respond to these cues by inviting children to extend the thinking: *It looks like you're agreeing with Lucy's thinking. What's making you think the same way?* Or, we might ask, *Are there other reasons this makes sense?* These are invitations to add another angle or new contextual support, and in doing so, begin developing a line of thinking.

Whether disagreement with an idea comes immediately, or builds slowly, the signs (as noted above) are usually obvious, and when we see them we might say *It sounds like you don't agree. What are you thinking?* And when a child offers a response, we might nudge a little more with *What makes you think that?* Disagreement not only can broaden thinking, it often signals the development of competing theories children must learn to navigate (discussed in Chapter Six).

When disagreement bubbles up, we have to decide at what point to work the dissent into the conversation. We might acknowledge it, have children who agree build their thinking as far as they can, and then start building off the disagreement. Or we might move back and forth between the two, nudging with comments such as *How is your thinking different?* or *Why do you think that is?*

Feedback for agreement and disagreement links the agreeing or disagreeing to the resulting depth and breadth of meaning. *When Ashley agreed with Stan, she added another reason why his idea made sense. This helped us to really explore the idea. So don't get frustrated when someone says what you were thinking. Remember, you can then build on to the idea and make it stronger.*

Or, in the case of disagreement, *When C.J. disagreed with Ellen about our character's actions, he offered his own insights. This helped us to ask more questions about the character's feelings, and think about the ways people behave differently for different reasons. Now we have a lot of wondering about the character to hold on to as we read more. Remember, disagreeing can be powerful when we're respectful and focused on growing ideas.*

Questioning

In her forward to *The World Café: Shaping Our Futures Through Conversations That Matter*, Margaret Wheatley speaks to the power of good questions: "Good questions help us become both curious and uncertain, and this is always the road that opens us to the surprise of new insight" (2005, xi).

Questions are a vital tool for exploring new possibilities. They allow us to clarify, of course, but with questions we can also request additional information or rationale, push against assumptions, and search out varied perspectives. That said, not all questions are created equally. Closed questions—those that funnel responses toward right answers—do little to engage children, or support constructing. These "right answer questions," particularly those that are scripted and begin with *Who can tell me . . .* , place the teacher in the controlling position and children in the role of pleasing the teacher as opposed to constructing collaboratively.

Questions with too much information embedded in them are equally counterproductive. When we lead with questions such as *Why do you think the character is sad?*, we've interpreted aspects of the text for children. When this happens, children tend to take our loaded questions, turn them into statements, add a bit, and hand them back to us. They may say things like *Yeah, he's really sad, because the other character was mean.* We celebrate, thinking that they've not only constructed understanding, but are also developing specific strategic abilities capable of transcending texts. In reality, though, what children are doing is restating and extending our understanding.

But everything shifts when questions are open and responsive to children's own thinking and talking. When framed to encourage reflection, tentativeness, exploration, and extended talk, these responsive questions have a kinetic energy all their own.

To encourage questions, we can **focus** children to be aware of their own wondering, confusion, or need to know more. We might say *As we talk today, when you notice that you're wondering about something in the text, someone's idea, what made them think a certain way, or if you want to know more about their idea, be sure to ask.*

To **facilitate**, we ask a range of responsive questions, modeling the types of questions the children themselves might ask to nudge the thinking forward. We might ask *why* questions: *But why do you think a person would do that?* Or we might ask *how* questions: *How could he have figured that out?* *What if* questions invite children to imagine different contexts and scenarios and work to apply reasoning. Or, questions may prompt a speaker to consider other interpretations or evidence: *But if he's really a good person, then why did he . . . ?* Or we consider other perspectives by asking *How might _____ think about this?* or perhaps *Are there other ways of thinking about that?*

Of course, **feedback** needs to show how the questions children asked impacted meaning making: *Harlan's idea surprised us, and many of you wanted to know more. You asked Harlan questions that pushed him to explain. As you listened, it helped us all to realize that there's more than one way to think about this issue. Paying attention to your thinking, noticing when you have a question, and asking that question are helpful moves to make.*

Bundling Thinking

As children clarify, agree and disagree, and question, they construct lines of thinking they need to hold on to as they continue to talk. But it can be challenging to clearly bundle all that thinking together, articulate it, and hold on to it.

To **focus** children on the need to bundle their thinking, we remind them of the challenge of holding on to and growing ideas if they don't pause now and again to gauge where they are. We might say, *Once we've done a lot of thinking and talking, let's make sure to pause and reflect on the bigger ideas that we're building. That will help us to hold on to them as we read and talk more.*

Then, **facilitation** that supports the bundling might sound like this: *Before we dive back into reading, let's consider where we are in our* *thinking. We seem to be thinking that our character is changing, but we're not quite sure why. Hold on to this wondering as we read a bit more, and see if we have new thoughts that help us understand better.* We have to "read" the conversation carefully and decide where it makes sense to pause and bundle the thinking before moving forward, remembering that when we do, we are teaching children how to do this same thing in their independent talk.

When we give **feedback,** we connect the deliberate pauses we took to verbalize our thinking to the difference they made in our efforts to grow that thinking: *Today, after we talked about the characters a bit, we took a moment to pull all of our thinking together. We realized we were all concerned about the way one of the characters was behaving. That helped us to focus on that character as we read more. Remember to push pause to pull thinking together any time you think it will help.*

Facilitative Language Shifts

The more children are aware of how talk enables them to grow ideas, the more they understand the *why* of purposeful talk. This understanding, or sense of purpose, propels their efforts as they think and talk with us— and without us. It's what helps children to make thoughtful decisions as they move in and out of alone time and partnership time during independent opportunities such as reading workshop, and in other arenas where thinking and talking purposefully with others matters.

The chart in Figure 5.2 summarizes some simple language shifts you can make as you facilitate the kind of children's talk that will help them as they work together to grow ideas.

Facilitative Language Shifts For Growing Ideas

Instead of saying...	Try saying this...
That's not what we're talking about.	*I wonder if this thought helps to grow the ideas we're exploring right now, or if this is one of those thoughts you might park on the side for later?* *How does that thought help with the ideas that we're building?* *Can you help us understand where that thought came from?*
You're not listening!	*Oh—that happens to me, too. I mean to listen, but my own thinking gets in the way. Here's what I do—I look at the person who was talking and say, "Will you please repeat that?"*
Be sure to listen!	*Let's listen closely to make sure we understand Amika's thinking.* *Listen to Diego's thinking and notice if it makes you wonder anything.*
Today, we're going to start talking about . . .	*Who thought more about our ideas last night? Did anyone's words linger with you? Is there a thought or idea that you can't let go of?*
That doesn't make sense.	*Kamal, do you mean . . . ?* *Can you say more about that?* *Letti, I think you're saying _____. Am I understanding you correctly?*
Good—who else has an idea? Who's next?	*What does Ari's idea have you thinking? How does this idea lie next to our earlier thinking?*
How many people agree? How many disagree?	*It looks like you're agreeing with Lucy's thinking. What's making you think the same way? Are there other reasons this makes sense?* *It sounds as if you don't agree. What are you thinking? What makes you think that?*
OK—good. My next question is . . .	*Why do you think . . .* *How could . . .* *But if . . .* *How might . . .*
Hold on to that thinking, and let's read on.	*So, we seem to be thinking that our character is changing, but we're not quite sure if that's true, or why it might be happening.* *Let's hold on to this wondering as we read a bit more, and see if we have new thoughts.*

What's the difference?	Transferring facilitation
This shifts us from judging and dismissing seemingly disconnected thinking to involving children in decisions about the constructive potential of their thought, or explaining their evolution of thought.	*Are you wondering what led Bobby to this thought? How might you ask him?*
Shifts us from scolding children for lapses in listening to developing their awareness of their own listening, and teaches strategies for remedying lapses in listening.	*How can we get ready to listen?* *What might you do if you realize your listening slipped?*
Shifts us away from telling children to listen. Offers suggestions for developing an active listening stance.	*What are you listening for?*
Shifts us from a parade of new text, new conversation each day to lingering inside books. Teaches the power of one aspect of reflec-tion—allowing someone's words to linger in our minds, "relistening" to them, and realizing greater potential in them.	*Are you wondering if anyone thought more about our ideas last night? How might you ask?*
Shifts us from dismissing confusing thinking to valuing and actively clarifying others' thoughts.	*Did anyone notice the look on Joey's face? Do you think he needs Hallie to say more about her thinking?* *If you're confused, what might you ask to help you understand?*
Shifts us away from a round-robin model of "talk as telling." Teach-es specific ways of lingering with a thought and working with it.	*How will you work with Ari's thinking?*
Shifts us from quick checking on agreement and disagreement as a "vote" to digging into agreement and disagreement for the purpose of deepening and broadening thinking.	*Should you explore other reasons why this makes sense?* *What will you do with different think-ing?*
Shifts us from pre-scripted questions to questions that genuinely respond to children's thoughts and meaning-making process and nudge for more.	*Why are you wondering about that thought?*
Shifts us away from an assumption that children have connected the bits of conversation into a meaningful whole. Supports a habit of pausing to bundle thinking into that meaningful whole.	*Where are we in our thinking? How do these pieces fit together? What should we hold on to as we read on?*

It is better to debate a question without settling it than to settle it without debate.

—Joseph Joubert

Six

Teaching Children to Negotiate Meaning

A Snapshot of Purposeful Talk

It's late in the school year, and I'm deep in conversation with a class of second graders who are stretching themselves as readers by immersing in books with complex characters, motives, and interactions. This is always some of my favorite work with readers, because, as we talk intently about characters, we're really exploring what it is to be human, coming to better understand ourselves, and learning to better empathize with and appreciate others.

The children are reading Nikki Grimes' powerful compilation of poems, *My Man Blue* (2002). With each poem, readers delve deeper into a developing relationship between a young man, Damon, and his Mom's long-ago friend, Blue. Damon, at least initially, isn't too happy about Blue's sudden presence in his life, and the second graders are scrambling to understand both Damon and Blue and the unsettled dynamic building between them.

The first poem introduced the children to Blue, and on this day, we are tackling the second poem, "When We First Met." Told through the perspective of Damon (whose name hasn't been introduced yet), this poem reveals his thoughts during his first uneasy encounter with Blue. As I finish reading, the children are uncharacteristically quiet. I look out at puzzled faces and tilted heads. The internal churning is palpable. I wait, and Brandon rewards my patience.

Brandon: I think like—he doesn't trust him.

Emma: Who?

Brandon: The boy. He thinks like, that guy's bad or something.

Manuel: And he's acting all tough to him.

Jamie: I think maybe he's—he's doing it 'cuz he's scared. He doesn't want Blue to be there.

Alania: But—wait. . . .

Alania looks perplexed. Something's tugging at her—something she can't quite articulate yet. She turns to me and asks, "Can you read it again?" A brilliant idea! Midway through the reread, as I finish the line, "'Cause in this family, *I'm* the only man," Alania jumps back in.

Alania: That part—it's why he's acting like he's all big stuff. He thinks—he thinks he has to be all tough and stuff. When it says the man—to be the man . . .

Desire: Like be grown up—and tough?

Alania: Yeah! [nodding in agreement]

Jonathan: But how Alania? He's a kid—he'd be scared.

Brandon: I'd be scared.

Rosie: Yeah—but look at how he is. He's giving attitude.

Maria: You mean in the illustration?

Rosie: [Nodding]

Jamie: Sometimes, when people act like that—it's—it's like, not—they're not really—they just act it.

Maria: That's interesting . . . why do you think people do that?

Tanya: It's faking. Maybe so we don't know how they are—if they're scared or something.

Rosie: Yeah, some people. But not him. See—he's got super attitude. And the mom says stop, 'cuz she knows . . .

And just like that, a carpet of quiet morphs into a lively negotiation as two theories about Damon's behavior emerge. A façade to hide fear, or an assertive stance to communicate control? Both theories are certainly possible, and in fact, both may have elements of truth.

The children push and pull between the two theories for a bit, exhausting their range of rationales to support each. They're unable to dismiss either theory, and a bit of frustration begins creeping in. "How can we tell?" Kaitlyn laments. It's quiet again as the group ponders this. Then, Lorali turns to me and asks, "What's the next poem? I think we need it now!"

There's so much to celebrate in this tiny bit of talk! Let's start with the range of voices joining the conversation. Without a turn and talk, and only a single clarifying comment from me, and in the span of but a few minutes, almost half the class weighs in. The others are nodding or shaking their heads and offering assorted "Yeahs!" and "Huhs?"

Nystrand's notion of uptake (1997)—thoughtfully and intentionally taking in the words of others, and responding to them in an effort to grow ideas—can be traced through the children's talk. As they grow ideas, two different theories about Damon are taking shape. There's an openness and earnestness to their process of reckoning. As they talk to strengthen one theory, they're also working to understand the rationale behind the other theory. Their thinking and talking are moving in and out of the text itself (using both the author's words and the illustrator's interpretation) and their own world, drawing on what they know about complex human emotions. Lorali's sudden push for the next poem is not impetuousness. Rather, it's a strategic, energized quest to propel the flow of meaning making forward.

Why Negotiating Meaning Matters

When children wrestle with complex ideas, multiple theories are bound to emerge—different ways of seeing ideas or situations that can be simultaneously compelling and perplexing. As these theories begin to build, we often hear comments such as "How can you think that!" and "No way, that doesn't make sense!" Peter Johnston says of this kind of disagreement, "For intellectual development, the most powerful lever comes when

> When children wrestle with complex ideas, multiple theories are bound to emerge—different ways of seeing ideas or situations that can be simultaneously compelling and perplexing.

children disagree and take each other seriously" (2012b, 65). His emphasis on children "taking each other seriously" is critical. The work of negotiating meaning is dependent on children's ability to listen with intent and follow each other's logic, but this can only happen if children are willing to talk about thinking they might disagree with (at least initially) and to try to understand that perspective as fully as possible. So, what we hope to hear alongside these expressions of incredulousness is some version of "Why do you think that?"

Sometimes, as children tussle between or among possibilities, one theory strengthens and eventually prevails. Other times, children end up agreeing to disagree. Either way, Ralph Peterson reminds us, "Through negotiation, students come to understand how someone else interprets an event, text, or situation; thereby, the basis for their own understanding is broadened" (1992, 81). Learning to navigate varied theories and perspectives prepares children for a world where they will need to think and talk daily with people who see things differently than they do. The more frequently children engage with difference, the more they come to expect varied interpretations and different perspectives.

> Learning to navigate varied theories and perspectives prepares children for a world where they will need to think and talk daily with people who see things differently than they do.

Working to see ideas or issues from all angles requires children to dwell in shades of gray. For many children, the resulting uncertainty can be unsettling. They look to us with pleas of "Can't you just tell us!" Dealing with difference can be particularly challenging for children who place a premium on "being right." When different perspectives challenge their way of thinking or their factual command of a topic, these children tend to dig in rather than engage.

For example, consider Joshua, a first grader whose confidence in his whale expertise was unwavering. His class was reading Eve Bunting's *Whales Passing* (2003), a gorgeous ode to orcas. Bunting explores the beauty of these mammals through the imaginative wonderings of a young boy and his father, who are watching a pod from cliffs high above the ocean. Their musings range from the orca's great migratory abilities to the ways whales touch the human spirit and engage the imagination.

When Bunting's young character asks, "How do they know which way to go?", Joshua sensed his moment. Rising to his knees, he began, "Oh—I know! It's echolocation. I read it—they do it from the blowhole. It's here [tapping the back of his head]. The whales, they make the sound. It's like sonar, and it bounces back, and then they know." The children listened, and even asked a few questions, which Joshua addressed gleefully and authoritatively.

As we read a bit more, Bunting's characters engaged in a mix of factual and mystical theorizing about a range of possible orca migratory behaviors, such as reading signposts, whale talk, and whale storytelling. At that point, Mai leaned in to get a closer look at the illustrations, and tentatively mused, "So maybe they do a bunch of things to know how to get there."

Joshua, however, wanted nothing to do with this expanded possibility. He immediately interjected, "No. I already said it. They use echolocation. I told you. They do it and bats, too, and . . . "

Mai looked to me, and then shrunk back, confidence in her tentative thought waning. But, if the children were to grasp the beauty and imagination of Bunting's work, revel in the awe she creates, and grasp the larger environmental and spiritual underpinnings of the text, Mai's tentative musings were exactly the direction in which their talk needed to go.

Joshua's unwillingness to entertain Mai's musings about whale migration stemmed at least partially, if not completely, from his belief that knowing lots of facts—and knowing them first and being right—is synonymous with being "smart." Our work with negotiating meaning includes helping children like Joshua open their minds to new possibilities and recognize that knowledge can deepen, broaden, or shift with new insights. We strive to develop both their willingness to be open to a range of thinking and their ability to engage with it flexibly, respectfully, and purposefully.

Teaching Talk Behaviors for Negotiating Meaning

The work of negotiating meaning may seem complex, but in truth, even our youngest learners can take first steps. Consider David Shannon's classic, *No, David!* (1998). Many a kindergartener will insist that David's mom is oh so angry, while others argue (perhaps from experience) that really, his mom is just a bit frustrated. With thoughtful instruction, these kindergarteners will grow into readers who are able to negotiate between and among increasingly complex aspects of their reactions to or interpretations of ideas in texts. What matters is that, right from the start, we focus on the importance of difference; that our facilitative stance is consistently open-minded, non-judgmental, and welcoming to the full range of possibility; and that we offer the feedback that makes the process and result of negotiating meaning visible.

Encouraging Difference

Because difference is a tool for both broadening and deepening thinking—as well as shifting thinking—we want to encourage a range of perspectives as children think and talk together. We can **focus** children on the importance of bringing difference into the conversation by saying something like: *As we talk together today, we know we're not all going to think the same way. When we listen to different ideas and talk about them, we always end up with even bigger ideas. So today, let's be sure to invite different thinking into the conversation to help us grow our thinking, and then really listen to it, even if we disagree.*

> **Because difference is a tool for both broadening and deepening thinking—as well as shifting thinking—we want to encourage a range of perspectives as children think and talk together.**

To **facilitate**, we actively invite different ways of thinking: *Does anyone have a different idea about this?* Or we look for shaking heads, frowns, or quizzical expressions as possible signs that children see things differently. We can nudge at this potential with comments such as: *It looks as if some of you aren't agreeing. What are you thinking?*

When I'm facilitating, I not only invite difference from the children themselves, but I also actively wonder about whose voice and different thinking might be missing from our conversation. I ask questions such as: *What would a parent think about this? How might people who live elsewhere think about this? What might the fifth graders down the hall think?* Doing this on a regular basis helps children develop a habit of actively seeking varied perspectives, as we saw with the trio in Chapter One thinking and talking about *Christmas in the Trenches*.

When we give **feedback**, we focus on the outcomes so children become more willing and able to invite difference into a conversation. We specifically link the active wondering about a different perspective, the thinking it introduced, and the result of that added thinking: *Juan, you wondered how younger kids might think about our character's actions. That wondering helped us realize that different people respond to actions in different ways. This made us realize that we can't just label our character as mean—it's more complicated than that. It's important to hold on to that kind of wondering in every conversation!*

Holding on to Competing Theories

As competing theories form, children may need support to consciously hold on to each theory and push and pull with them as they continue to read on and construct understanding.

We **focus** children on the importance of holding on to theories by reminding them that differences may emerge, and that as we read and talk more, we'll want to revisit each theory and think it through using new insights. *We've noticed that, as we talk, we sometimes have more than one idea or theory about what's happening and why. We know we need to keep talking about these theories. So, we have to hold all of them in our heads.*

To help children hold on to multiple theories, the first **facilitation** move is to pause the conversation and make sure the developing theories are visible to all. We say something like: *So, I'm hearing two different ways of thinking. Ava is helping us to consider that ____. But, some of you are thinking that ____.* Then, once the ideas are visible to all, we remind children to keep them front and center in their minds as we read and talk more: *Let's take a moment and let our two theories settle in our minds. Now, let's hold on to both of these as we read more and talk more.*

The **feedback** we give needs to point to the importance of holding on to the theories as we move forward: *As we read on today, Jake was holding both theories in the front of his mind. Because of this, he realized when something we read strengthened one theory and pushed against the other. He stopped us so we could all talk about it, and we all agreed that one theory wasn't making a lot of sense anymore. So, holding on to theories like this really helps when we're wrestling with different ways of thinking about our ideas.*

Talking Between Theories

Once we have articulated multiple theories and children are consciously holding on to them, we have to show students how to talk and think—to negotiate—between or among them.

To **focus** children's attention on the need to actively negotiate between or among theories, we remind them of the value of this negotiation: *When we realize that we're seeing an idea or issue in different ways, working to understand both ways seems to help us to be open-minded and sometimes sparks new thinking. Today, if different theories are building, let's talk between them, and notice what happens!*

Facilitation then begins with helping children to seriously consider each possibility. We say things such as *Let's focus on this idea first, and then we can dig into the other.* This requires the children who may be leaning in one direction or the other to suspend their developing stance and remain open to possibilities. To encourage open minds, I often nudge children to explore potential reasons for different ways of thinking by asking, *Why might we be thinking differently about this?* We then explore the reasons for disagreement, ranging from varied life experiences to different interpretations of actions or words, and numerous other possibilities.

If I sense frustration with the shades of gray, I acknowledge the frustration by saying something like: *You know, I'm struggling a bit. Both ways of thinking (or all three ways of thinking) have bits that make sense to me. Is anyone else feeling this way? I'm going to just keep holding on to all the ways of thinking as we keep reading and talking. If I do that, I think I'll begin to figure out which idea seems strongest to me.* Then as we read more and talk more, I am alert to whether or not children are connecting their new thinking to the different theories on the table, often prompting, *How does this thinking connect to the theories we're holding on to?*

The **feedback** we give should make the children's process visible and tie it to the resulting meaning making. We might say: *Today, we realized we were building two different ways of thinking about what was happening with our character. As we read, Bree noticed that our character's feelings seemed to be changing, and asked how that affected both ways of thinking. That reminded us to talk more about each theory. As we talked more about each, one theory didn't seem to make as much sense anymore. We think we're a little closer to really understanding this character now. This is why talking between theories is important.*

Remaining Flexible

To engage in a serious negotiation of meaning, we have to remain flexible and be willing to allow our own thinking to shift. To **focus** children on this, we ready them to be open-minded, and we develop a culture that makes changing minds a normal part of the process of constructing meaning. *As we think and talk, sometimes we notice that our first way of thinking doesn't feel quite right anymore. That means we're really listening to new thoughts and different ideas and considering new possibilities. This really expands our understanding.*

Facilitation that develops and supports flexible thinking begins with helping children use the constructive flow of conversation to continually assess the strength and validity of differing theories. I sometimes make comments such as, *Wow, I didn't agree with that at first, but now I'm thinking. . . .* This makes my own flexible stance visible. I often follow up by asking, *Is anyone else feeling their thinking shifting?* Or I might nudge by saying, *I wonder if the theory Jocelyn and Rob were developing still makes sense?*

When we give **feedback,** we're careful to normalize flexibility as part of the process of understanding. *As we read, you paused and used new understandings to help you think more about the theories we've been holding on to. Anthony noticed that the idea he thought made the most sense* *wasn't really making sense anymore, and he began to lean more toward a different theory. This willingness to be flexible means his thinking was able to keep growing. We need to be flexible like this in every conversation.*

Finding Value in Difference

In truth, our greatest leap in learning often comes when we open our minds to different ways of thinking. As they experience negotiating meaning, children grow to see that engaging with difference is an important lever for deepening and broadening meaning making, but we don't want to leave this development to chance. Pointing out the value of difference is a critical part of teaching children to negotiate meaning.

We **focus** children by reminding them of the value of thinking and talking between or among theories: *Yesterday, when we were pushing and pulling with the different theories you had about our character, a brand new idea began to form. If we hadn't worked so hard to understand both theories, that never would have happened! Let's work to keep an open mind like that again today.*

> ❝ *In truth, our greatest leap in learning often comes when we open our minds to different ways of thinking.* ❞

Then, as we **facilitate**, we are careful to comment on the effects of different perspectives on our own thinking. *Wow, I never considered that some people might look at this in that way.* Or sometimes we're more specific. *Isn't it interesting how we interpret this character's actions in different ways? That helps me to realize there may be more going on here than I first thought.*

Our **feedback** needs to be very specifically tied to the value of seeking difference in meaning making. *I noticed how willing you were to consider other ways of thinking today. When you disagreed with Courtney, but still asked her about her thinking, you began to realize that this issue might be more complex than you realized at first. Digging deeply into a different idea, even though it didn't make sense to you at first, proved to really matter. We need to always keep an open mind like that.*

Educating for Democracy

The value of wading into shades of gray, dwelling in difference, and working between theories actually goes far beyond deepening meaning. To explain why, I'll share a conversation from my book *Comprehension*

Through Conversation (2006), along with Peter Johnston's important take on it.

Reading workshop in my second- and third-grade classrooms was in full swing, and as I conferred, I was becoming increasingly aware of an animated conversation unfolding between Manny and Sergio. The two were deeply engaged in reading Eve Bunting's *A Picnic in October* (2004), a touching story that explores a multi-generational immigrant family through the eyes of two young boys. In the story, the boys reluctantly join their grandmother for the family's annual pilgrimage to Ellis Island to honor the birthday of the Statue of Liberty. It's a ritual the characters struggle to understand, and their disconnect leads to rambunctious behavior, which had been providing rich fodder for Manny and Sergio's thinking.

As their talk increased in fervor, I could no longer resist. I pulled up next to the partnership as Manny was explaining his perspective about the boys' behavior.

> Manny: No, no, you see, he was rude but he changed.
>
> Sergio: Rude people don't change. He was making fun of everyone; he pretended to throw up . . .
>
> Manny: That's sick!
>
> Sergio: Yea, but it was because he didn't want to go, he was like mad they made him . . . and embarrassed, too, like me when my mom makes me go . . .
>
> Manny: Yeah, at first, but look here at the end, see [flips the pages]—they're leaving . . . here it is, see, he looks, he looks at the other family—it's like he gets it!
>
> Sergio: Let me see again [grabs book, studies the pictures on the pages Manny showed him and whisper-reads the words on the pages]. Oh—you mean like now he gets why the Grandma thinks the statue is a big deal?
>
> Manny: Yeah, now he gets it.
>
> Sergio: So now it's in his heart, too?
>
> Manny: No—well, OK, yeah, I guess it could be in his heart, but now he really gets that it's in his Grandma's heart. (2006, 91)

As they lingered over this text, Manny and Sergio had constructed different theories about Bunting's characters. They were actively negotiating between these theories, listening thoughtfully, pushing and pulling using the text itself and their understanding of the world to see each other's perspective. Sergio maintained a flexible stance, and seemed to be slowly shifting toward Manny's way of seeing.

In reflecting on this conversation, Peter Johnston connects Manny and Sergio's ability to negotiate meaning to the bigger work of becoming active, engaged citizens. Johnston points out that:

> These children and their peers are learning to participate in a strong democracy. They expect to engage, to disagree, and to grow from that disagreement. At some point, they will vote, but that will be after they have understood their own and each other's views and have expanded their collective mind in the process. Even if they vote self-interest, it will be enlightened self-interest. (2012b, 6)

Johnston's reflections remind us that the work of teaching children to talk together purposefully has lifelong impact. It matters in our children's lives, and in the world they will be a part of creating.

Too, Johnston's reflections remind us of the reciprocity between talk and community. We can continue to strengthen negotiation and help children value it by weaving it into the democratic life in our classroom. For example, if we are working through disagreement in a class meeting, we might **focus** children on their growing ability to use talk as a tool: *As we figure this out, let's think about how important being a flexible thinker is. We know we can listen and work to understand even if we don't agree.* Then, we **facilitate** that conversation by drawing from the very same facilitative language we've already explored, and offer **feedback** that helps children link the ability to negotiate difference to the continual strengthening of our community.

Facilitative Language Shifts

The more willing children are to embrace difference and negotiate between or among theories, the more they become capable, independent learners. But learning to embrace difference takes time, thoughtful support, and patience. Even if, in the end, children agree to disagree, the time and effort that goes into negotiating difference has a huge payoff. The chart in Figure 6.1 summarizes some facilitative language shifts you can use to help children learn to negotiate meaning.

Facilitative Language Shifts For Negotiating Meaning

Instead of saying...	Try saying this...
That's an interesting thought. Let's keep reading . . .	*Does anyone have a different idea about this?* *It looks as if some of you aren't agreeing. What are you thinking?*
OK, so we think . . .	*What would a parent think about this? How might people who live elsewhere think about this? What might the fifth graders down the hall think?*
I hear two different ideas, and I think . . .	*So, we're not all thinking the same thing. Take a moment and let the range of thinking settle in your mind.* *I'm hearing two different ways of thinking. Ava is helping us to consider that _____. But some of you are thinking that _____.* *Let's focus on this idea first, then we can dig into the other.* *Now, let's hold on to both of these as we read more and talk more.*
I think that idea only came up because . . . *What we need to focus on is . . .*	*What might be causing the differences in our thinking?*
This is hard and it's taking a long time. Let's settle on . . .	*You know, I'm struggling a bit. Both ways of thinking have bits that make sense to me. Is anyone else feeling that way? I'm going to keep holding on to both ways of thinking as we keep reading and talking.*
Any new ideas? Good—let's move on now.	*How does this thinking connect to the theories we're currently holding on to?*
That's interesting, but I already made up my mind.	*Wow, I didn't agree with that at first, but now, I'm thinking . . .*
No one would think that!	*Wow, I never considered that some people might look at this in that way.* *Isn't it interesting how we interpret characters' words in different ways? That helps me to realize there may be more going on here than I first thought.*

Figure 6.1 Facilitative Language Shifts for Negotiating Meaning

What's the difference?	Transferring facilitation
This shifts us from settling for a single perspective to actively inviting varied perspectives. The invitation not only opens the door for other perspectives, but also immediately dispels any sense of a single "right" way of seeing things.	*Do you think some of us might be thinking differently about this? How could you ask?*
Shifts us from considering the perspectives of only those who are present to considering the perspectives of voices not currently represented.	*Who might think differently about this? How might you find out . . . ?*
Shifts us from the identifier and holder of multiple ways of thinking and person responsible for orchestrating talk between or among that thinking, to children developing independence with recognizing and talking among multiple theories.	*So, what ideas are we considering at this point?* *How should we think and talk more about these theories?* *What should we hold on to as we keep reading?*
Shifts us from a sense of "right" or "wrong" ways of thinking toward an understanding that different ways of seeing emerge from different interpretations, life experiences, and background knowledge. Develops an expectation of, as well as a value for, differing perspectives.	*Are you curious about the differences in thinking?* *What could you ask to help explore them?*
Shifts us away from a need to form fast and firm opinions and toward open-mindedness and a willingness to tolerate ambiguity while constructing understanding.	*What uncertainties are you holding on to?*
Shifts us from thoughts in isolation to an understanding that meaning continually evolves, and that new thinking has the potential to shift previous understandings.	*How is this new thinking helping you?*
Shifts us from fast and firm answers/opinions, and further strengthens the understanding that meaning continually evolves, and that new thinking has the potential to shift previous understandings. Emphasizes the power of open-mindedness and flexibility.	*How will you get your mind ready for another way of thinking?*
Shifts us away from an expectation that everyone sees things the same way we do and toward recognition of different ways of seeing things. Develops value for the potential of different ways of seeing to broaden and deepen thinking.	*What thinking surprised you? How will you use it?*

A full-size version of this table can be downloaded from http://hein.pub/biggerideas (click on Companion Resources).

Look closely.

The beautiful may

be small.

—Immanuel Kant

Seven

Assessing Purposeful Talk

A Snapshot of Purposeful Talk

"But, why did they tell it again?"

Thinking back to Chapter Two, you may remember this question—Lawrence's question—that launched the extended exploration of ideas from *A Kitten Called Moonlight*. As the ensuing talk began to dwindle, I found myself in one of those decision-making moments common to teaching into process-oriented work. Should I continue to support Lawrence through facilitated whole-class talk, or should I invite him to continue thinking and talking with a greater degree of independence during reading workshop?

I mulled this briefly, and then handed the book over to Lawrence. This decision wasn't a whim, though. Rather, it was a deliberate move, based on a carefully constructed understanding of his growing abilities with talk and meaning making, and the encouraging way his community rallied around him.

I knew Lawrence tended to be contemplative by nature, and that we didn't often hear his voice in the whole group. But I was also becoming aware of a shift. Lawrence had started joining in on the talk a little more often, and when he did, the conversations raging in his mind crept out, leaving no doubt that he had been thinking alongside his classmates. In smaller groups and partnerships, Lawrence was becoming noticeably more verbal, actively engaging out loud with little to no prompting.

Too, the way Lawrence's classmates took on his query both warmed my heart and had my kidwatching radar in overdrive. These children were not only internalizing talk behaviors, they were also showing evidence they understood the constructive intent behind them. Given all that I'd been noticing and considering, I decided a compelling text and the opportunity to engage independently with peers seemed an ideal option for Lawrence.

Keeping the Goal in Mind

The dynamic nature of teaching purposeful talk situates us continuously in decision-making mode. Sometimes we're able to be contemplative about the decisions, as when we're designing instruction and selecting texts. At other times, such as this pivot point with Lawrence, we're making in-the-moment decisions.

> *When it comes to assessing purposeful talk, one of the 'big things' we need to stay focused on is our children's individual and collective trajectory toward the goal of purposeful talk—the ability to think and talk to 'get to a place that you just can't get to in one mind.'*

When it comes to decision-making, whether contemplative or in-the-moment, author and futurist Alvin Toffler thoughtfully asserts, "You've got to think about big things while you're doing small things so that all the small things go in the right direction."

When it comes to assessing purposeful talk, one of the "big things" we need to stay focused on is our children's individual and collective trajectory toward the goal of purposeful talk—the ability to think and talk to "get to a place that you just can't get to in one mind." Our understanding of this trajectory is what guides our decisions, including seemingly small ones such as handing a book off to Lawrence. As we think about assessing with this goal in mind, it may be helpful to return to the expanded definition of purposeful talk I first offered in Chapter One. Purposeful talk:

★ **honors constructive intent** as it engages participants in a deliberate process of building on a range of thinking to construct unique ideas, strategize, and innovate. Participants recognize their ability to draw from what Peter Senge describes as "a 'larger pool of meaning,' accessible only to a group" (1990, 248), and believe deeply in the value of doing so.

★ *harnesses the power of varied perspectives* to broaden and deepen the thinking and constructive potential of a conversation. Participants value the differing perspectives, actively seek them out, and work to fully understand each voice.

★ *engages participants over expanded time and space.* Purposeful talk honors the time participants need to deepen and evolve understanding. Participants recognize that the process of constructing doesn't necessarily happen in simple, quick conversations. They're willing to dwell in shades of gray as they wrestle with varied perspectives, contemplate possibilities, and gather new thinking. They recognize that compelling ideas may linger and evolve over time, and are willing to cycle back to rethink and revise or expand previous understandings.

Because the goal of purposeful talk is to construct meaning, assessing children's talk absent of meaning making simply doesn't make sense. Yet, too many assessment tools distill complex talk down into simplistic, easy-to-capture bits of the whole. With talk, quantity is the easiest bit to capture, so quantity-driven talk checklists thrive. These checklists do provide ready data, adeptly tracking who talked and how often, but is this the most meaningful data?

> ❝ Because the goal of purposeful talk is to construct meaning, assessing children's talk absent of meaning making simply doesn't make sense. ❞

If we had used a talk checklist to assess the whole of Lawrence and his classmates' conversation about *A Kitten Called Moonlight*, we would have noted several children who added their voices many, many times over. These more verbal children would certainly have captured our attention, and they would each have had lots of checkmarks. With deeper inspection, however, we would no doubt see that these voices sometimes added thoughtfully to the conversation, but at other times were commenting or repeating in ways that didn't have quite the same impact.

However, Lawrence, who added his voice just once, asked a question that seemed to resonate and launch a new phase of meaning making. He constructed his question internally as he listened intently to the conversation. How do we capture this on a tool designed to quantify? Do fewer checkmarks mean less ability to use talk to construct? Do they help us to understand patterns of participation over time, or the ways the group as a whole uses talk to construct together? As an added challenge, if children realize we're tracking the quantity of their talk, they'll talk a lot—whether they make meaningful contributions or not. Talking with the intent to construct then gets lost in the urgency to say as much as possible as often as possible.

Other types of checklists are designed to document specific talk behaviors and etiquette, and they can be handy tools for noting whether or not children are making eye contact, asking questions, agreeing, disagreeing, and so on. Unfortunately, these checklists only confirm the use—or lack of use—of the behaviors and etiquette. They don't focus our attention on the purposefulness of children's talk and the ways it engages them in meaning making.

Rather than quantifying talk, or checking off children's use of specific behaviors, we need to focus instead on children's use of purposeful talk to construct meaning. But what exactly are we listening and looking for? Let's think through a stance to focus our attention, and a few possible lenses to unpack what we're hearing and seeing.

Developing an Inquiry Mindset for Assessment

The root of the word *assessment* comes from the Latin *assidere*, which means "to sit beside." As children think and talk, sitting beside them is exactly where we need to be. We pull up close and keep our eyes and our ears focused. And as we do, the key to gathering richly meaningful assessment data is to keep an inquiry mindset—alert and always poised to learn from the talk unfolding around us.

> *The key to gathering richly meaningful assessment data is to keep an inquiry mindset—alert and always poised to learn from the talk unfolding around us.*

Of course, children need to be talking, and talking a lot, for this mindset to yield its riches. Peter Johnston points out that, "Noticing what children know and can do, and how they understand literacy, is easier when their literate learning is accessible (visible and audible). This means that children need to read and write a lot and to talk about doing so in ways that provide information about their development" (2003, 91).

When children are engaged in an honest flow of talk, we gain an authentic sense of their ability to construct through talk, and we can actually experience the ways a child's thinking grows and changes in response to others' thinking. This is *real* data. But not all kinds of talk offer this portal into children's processing. If we control the talk too much or steer the meaning making to our own ends, we lose the opportunity to meaningfully assess. You may remember the first graders from Chapter Two who were talking about *A Pocket Full of Kisses*. If you look back you will see that, even with their conversation recorded word for word, there just isn't much to learn about their ability with talk because they were using talk to answer questions, not construct deeper understanding.

> **When children are engaged in an honest flow of talk, we gain an authentic sense of their ability to construct through talk, and we can actually experience the ways a child's thinking grows and changes in response to others' thinking. This is real data.**

Because an honest flow of talk is so incredibly dynamic, it's challenging to look and listen closely, especially when facilitating with a whole group. It helps to gather a general sense of the ways the children are constructing together, and then focus in on a few specific children. The children I tune in to on a given day, or over several consecutive days, may be those actively engaged in a particularly fascinating bit of talk, children I'm particularly curious about, or children like Lawrence who are exhibiting unexpected talk behaviors.

After a whole-class conversation, I'll take a few minutes to make notes on these children, quickly scribbling thoughts, wonderings, or bits of talk that are echoing in my head. Or I may use an audio or video recording, gathering longer bits of talk to unpack at a later point.

When children are thinking and talking together in more independent pursuits, such as reading workshop, I'll listen and watch a bit before I begin conferring. To help me hold on to what I'm seeing and hearing, I'll take notes and capture bits of conversation, allowing me to later tease out specifics in the flow of talk and other aspects of the social interaction. And at times I may again opt to actually record talk through audio or video to unpack and analyze later in greater depth.

As I sit alongside children to assess their talk, the first thing I do is note the particular context in which the talk is happening, because context matters. Are the children I'm observing talking in a facilitated situation? Are they talking as a whole class, in small groups, or partnerships? Or are they thinking and talking in un-facilitated small groups or partnerships? Are they talking about a previous read-aloud where a first phase of meaning making was actively facilitated? Or are the children thinking and talking about a new text? Is this a first conversation about the ideas or issues, or are children lingering with the text, or thinking across texts? Are they in assigned partnerships or navigating their own flow in and out of talk with self-selected partners? All of this information factors into thoughtful assessment of what I'm hearing and seeing.

After noting the context, I watch and listen with five overarching questions in mind. These questions help me tune in and focus on what children know *about* talk, how they're constructing *through* talk, and the extent to which they own this process:

★ What range of talk behaviors am I noticing, and how purposeful are they?

★ What individual and collective patterns of participation am I noticing?

★ What is the strength of the community around the talk?

★ What is the strength of the resulting meaning making?

★ How much facilitation is needed?

To help us think about how these questions can guide our assessment of purposeful talk, let's return to just a brief bit of the conversation that spun out of Lawrence's question about *A Kitten Called Moonlight*. It's powerful to see how, with focused questions to guide us, we can learn so much from looking closely and thinking deeply about just a little bit of talk.

Lawrence: But, why did they tell it again?

Eric: Families really do it. So they remember their good times.

Brenda: Yeah—because my family does it.

Kendra: Telling stuff? What . . .

Brenda: [Picking up the line of thinking before Kendra is able to finish her question] My mom—she tells about how when we're little— the stuff we did.

Eric: Yeah—so you can remember it.

Rosa: And so they—all of them knows it's special together.

Jamika: Yeah—see [pointing toward the book]. On the cover—how they are when they tell it.

Rosa: Yeah—special. It's how the mom and the girl are together.

What Range of Talk Behaviors Am I Noticing, and How Purposeful Are They?

Although we don't want to assess talk behavior separately from meaning making, it is helpful to note the range of behaviors children are using as they construct. This helps us gauge what children are learning about talk. I hold on to several lines of inquiry as I watch and listen:

★ Which talk behaviors am I noticing?

★ What purpose do they seem to be serving?

★ Am I seeing this behavior in all children, or just specific individuals?

★ Am I noticing a difference between facilitated talk behaviors and independent talk behaviors? In what way?

My Assessment

When I look closely at this bit of talk from the six children, I see that they were genuinely constructing meaning as they worked to understand why the characters in *A Kitten Called Moonlight*—and through the characters, the people in their own lives—behave the way they do. They were lingering with an aspect of the text that resonated, and their thoughts connected meaningfully. These thoughts are evidence of listening, as each was responsive to the building line of reasoning. To keep this line of thinking alive, the children both questioned and agreed, adding context from their experiences with their own families. We see Kendra making a move to clarify Brenda's thought about her family, enabling the context Brenda added to bring new perspective to the conversation—an addition that was clearly valued.

There's no negotiation at this point because differing theories had not emerged—at least, not yet. This is something to watch for as the children wade deeper into meaning with this text, explore these ideas across texts, or simply engage in other conversations.

Although I did not lean in to facilitate during this exchange, the conversation did spring from a larger conversation that was facilitated and did involve many more voices. Would this type of extended exchange have happened if these individuals had been thinking and talking with a text in small groups or partnerships without previous teacher facilitation? Something to watch for in reading workshop!

What Individual and Collective Patterns of Participation Am I Noticing?

As we watch and listen to children's talk, we hope to see evidence that each child recognizes the importance of his or her own voice in constructing big ideas. But we also know that we won't hear every voice out loud in every conversation. Children, just like adults, have unique patterns of participation.

To understand any one child's pattern of participation, we have to watch and listen to that child over time. This pushes against any temptation to rely on a snapshot of talk behavior. A child's participation may vary with different texts and ideas, different groupings, and on different days. Holding on to this keeps us from over-reacting to a bad day, or a text that falls short, or ideas that resonate for some but not for all. Lines of inquiry I tend to hold on to are:

★ What am I noticing about children's participation in the talk?

★ Is this usual or unusual? Why might that be?

★ What am I noticing in the quieter children? Do I see signs of active, in-the-head engagement?

★ How are the "talk early, talk often" children balancing talking and listening?

★ How do varied groupings or partnerships affect individual and collective participation in talk?

★ Am I noticing a difference in participation between facilitated talk and independent talk? In what way?

My Assessment

Lawrence's question was actually a bit of a surprise, because at one point in time he would have kept that question locked inside. His willingness not only to ask, but also to ask despite the fact that the group was moving on, shows the depth of his inner engagement, his trust in his community, and his developing understanding of the power of talk. My question about Lawrence now becomes *Why?* Why did the question come out this time? Is it growth in talk behavior alone, or is it a compelling need to know that he just couldn't suppress—or both?

Another surprise in this conversation was Brenda. While more apt to join into whole-group conversation than Lawrence, she rarely did so without an invitation. Yet this time she chimed in on her own, eagerly adding her thoughts. My questions about Brenda now echo my questions about Lawrence. Is she developing the realization that her voice matters—that she has a perspective that might support others?

Eric, on the other hand, tends to talk early and often. We've been working on taking in thinking from others—and I see signs of progress in this bit of talk. He actually made space for three turns between his first and second thoughts, and three more after! By taking a listening stance, he allowed Brenda to join in, and the context she brought to the conversation deepened the meaning making. His second addition to the conversation was building on Brenda's thinking and confirming his own, a sign that he's intently engaged with the developing thinking. Kendra, Rosa, and Jamika have all developed a thoughtful flow between listening to draw thinking in and adding their own voice, and I see this pattern continuing.

Then, I'm curious about the numerous voices in the class that didn't lean back into this conversation. There was a seriousness to the work that transcended the whole of the class. I had the sense that all were listening, following the flow of ideas. Granted, the talk was quick. Too, I didn't offer the support of facilitation (mostly because these six were engaged in an honest flow of talk without me). I can't help but wonder, did their classmates realize that hearing from both Lawrence and Brenda was unusual? Was I perhaps seeing respect for valued community members? These are fascinating new questions to carry forward!

What Is the Strength of the Community Around the Talk?

For learning to truly float on a sea of talk, children must feel that their voices are welcomed and valued and that efforts to collaborate are sincere and meaningful. To assess the strength of the learning community, I'm always watchful, noting how children are responding to one other. When someone speaks, I look and listen for signs of respect, or the lack of it. I may notice that children are listening with intent, or that side conversations are erupting as others are talking. I might hear a welcoming tone in children's voices—or not. I may note a willingness to wait a bit while a child works to put his thinking into words, or others jumping in without concern. I may hear invitations to add new perspectives or see eyes rolling in response to different thinking. All of this information helps me to support children in growing their community, and through this community, their talk. The lines of inquiry I hold on to include these following questions:

★   Do children seem to value each other's thoughts?

★   How are children supporting each other as they construct meaning?

★   How do varied groupings or partnerships affect this?

★   Am I noticing a difference in community support between facilitated talk and independent talk? In what way?

My Assessment

One of the first things that caught my attention was the way Lawrence's classmates responded to his question. As noted in Chapter Two, the other children could easily have dismissed it, either because they had already discussed the mother and daughter's retelling of their story, or because they were anxious to move on to their own reading. Instead, Lawrence's classmates listened, understood the earnestness of his question, and responded on their own. The simple fact that they didn't wait for me says a lot about who owns the learning!

Kendra's request for more information from Brenda not only honors her input, but shows genuine interest, and a realization that Brenda's perspective has value. Eric and Rosa imagine themselves into

Brenda's world with their own rationale for her family's behavior. This is not only critical for building meaning and empathy, but also a perfect example of the ways talk draws community members closer.

As I handed the book off to Lawrence, he settled in, and Brenda, Kaya, and Issy made their way over to join him. Others stopped in at varied points to listen or add a thought. I had a hunch that Brenda's connection with her own family had her intrigued—perhaps to the point of captivation—so I wasn't surprised to see her head over to join Lawrence. I was curious about Kaya and Issy. They tended to partner in reading workshop and had been engaged in an exploration of anything and everything that had to do with sea otters. What enticed them away? Lawrence's earnestness and a desire to support him? Intrigue at Brenda's connection? The lure of compelling ideas? I could hardly wait to ask!

What Is the Strength of the Resulting Meaning Making?

And because I just can't say it often enough, we simply can't separate talk from meaning making. As I'm noting talk behavior, patterns of participation, and community support, I'm listening intently to the depth and breadth of meaning the children are constructing. If the talk sounds good on the surface, but children aren't constructing ideas, something's amiss. It may be that they've learned phrasing for talk behaviors, or are using talk stems without having internalized the intent of the talk. So, the lines of inquiry I hold on to are these following questions:

★ What depth and breadth of understanding are children constructing? How does this relate to their talk? How does this relate to their cognitive strategy work?

★ How might their meaning making be broadened or deepened?

★ As children think and talk independently, are they moving from individual exploration to collaboration thoughtfully?

★ As children think and talk independently, are they lingering with single texts to strengthen understanding?

★ As children think and talk independently, are they pursuing ideas across multiple texts?

My Assessment

Even in this little bit of talk, I can see that Lawrence and his friends are heavily engaged in constructing meaning. They're clearly lingering in text, and doing so purposefully as they continue building bigger ideas. As they question motives and make connections, they're imagining themselves into the mother and daughter's minds to understand their interaction, and drawing from their own lives to understand the characters. We could easily unpack a range of comprehension strategies in their process—strategies they draw from independently and thoughtfully. This strategy work, combined with their talk, is enabling them to develop a theory about the way families use memories to bond, drawing parallels between the characters and their own families. Collectively, they're using their lives to understand the text, and then the text to help them better understand their lives—constructing a bigger understanding than a single mind might have built alone.

How Much Facilitation Is Needed?

As we focus children on talk, facilitate that talk, and offer feedback, we're providing models of effective talk and meaning making, and nudging students toward greater independence with it. As I'm working with children, I'm consistently noting what kinds of facilitative support they're still needing, and how much of it. Lines of inquiry I consider include these questions:

*   ★   What aspect(s) of talk behavior need facilitating?
*   ★   What aspect(s) of the meaning making need facilitating?
*   ★   How much facilitating?
*   ★   In what contexts?
*   ★   For all children, or specific individuals?

If I'm able to actually record a whole-class or small-group conversation, I can think even more specifically about my facilitative moves and add a new dimension to the assessment opportunity. With this closer look, I can ask other questions, such as:

★ Is my facilitation invitational, responsive, agentive, and meaning-driven?

★ Does my facilitation seem to be enough, too much, or not enough?

★ Are there places where I might have handed off some of the facilitation moves to the children?

My Assessment

In this particular bit of talk from *A Kitten Called Moonlight*, I wasn't facilitating. However, this talk was an expansion of a facilitated conversation where there was some support in the form of text selection and meaning making. I had nudged the children to keep lines of thinking about the mother and child's interactions alive, hoping they might develop theories about why the retelling of the story was so important.

However, what was truly interesting was that the children needed *no* facilitation in the little bit of talk that supported Lawrence's question. As I usually did, I had been watching both Lawrence and Brenda, two of the quieter voices, throughout the read-aloud. I constantly wrestled with whether or not to create space for their voices and invite them in, nudge other children to invite them in, or just watch to see at what point their own internal thinking might compel them to speak. I had held back this day, and was actually questioning my decision when out of nowhere came Lawrence, with Brenda close behind. This assessment is a good reminder that sometimes, holding back to see what children can do without us is wise.

Using Assessment to Make Thoughtful Instructional Decisions

Robin Alexander so eloquently reminds us that "the acts of teaching and assessing are intimately connected" (2008, 33). Sitting beside children, watching and listening closely as they talk, offers us incredible insights and helps us to be thoughtful as we plan our focus, facilitate, and feedback cycles of instruction. We have a keener sense of which aspects of talk behavior and meaning making need added focus and facilitation, or when we may need to angle our feedback in a particular direction. Essentially, we gather the information we need to maintain a forward trajectory with purposeful talk—and meaning making—over time.

As both Lawrence and Brenda added their voices, I realized that each child had developed a degree of confidence and begun to recognize the power of their contributions. To support them both, my feedback needs to touch on the constructive power of Lawrence realizing that the questions in his head were too loud to let go of, the value of him putting his question back into the circle for all to consider, and the importance of the perspective Brenda's voice added.

Eric, whose voice tended to be more prominent in conversations, needs feedback on developing his flow between listening and talking. I need to help him connect the space he gave to others to the powerful construction of understanding.

And, of course, I'm thinking about the ways the ideas compelled two usually quiet, contemplative talk personalities, and am curious about where else we might go with these ideas. Should we continue building on ideas about family, ritual and shared story by reading books by other authors, such as Patricia Polacco, Tomie dePaola, or Angela Johnson? Should I just suggest this, or would it be better to do a few book talks to see if anyone is drawn in this direction during independent reading?

As I assess children's abilities to think and talk together, it's important to note that "talk mastery" isn't part of my inquiry. Learning *about* and *through* purposeful talk is continuous. I'm constantly noticing, wondering, and working toward thoughtful decisions, including the small decisions, that keep children on a forward trajectory toward the goal of thinking and talking to "get to a place that you just can't get to in one mind." And as children get better and better at purposeful talk, I can keep moving this goal post, encouraging and supporting them to use talk to explore ever more complex ideas.

> **The process of building bigger ideas through purposeful talk requires slowing down, tuning in to an honest flow of talk, and listening and looking closely.**

The process of building bigger ideas through purposeful talk requires slowing down, tuning in to an honest flow of talk, and listening and looking closely. Sometimes what we hear and see wows us. Meaning making that far surpasses expectations. Long runs of talk without any need for facilitation. At other times, the beauty is more subtle—a slightly longer than usual exchange, an unexpected voice, or a child who just won't let a conversation end. Seeing this and knowing how to use it fuel our teaching in ways that checkmarks never will.

To support your efforts, the overarching questions and lines of inquiry I draw from are reprinted in Figure 7.1. This document can be reproduced to keep beside you, guiding your inquiry.

Assessing Purposeful Talk

Five Overarching Questions	Lines of Inquiry
What range of talk behaviors am I noticing, and how purposeful are these behaviors?	• Which talk behaviors am I noticing? • What purpose do they seem to be serving? • Am I seeing this behavior in all children, or just specific individuals? • Am I noticing a difference between facilitated talk behaviors and independent talk behaviors? In what way?
What individual and collective patterns of participation am I noticing?	• What am I noticing about children's participation in the talk? • Is this usual or unusual? Why might that be? • What am I noticing in the quieter children? Do I see signs of active, in-the-head engagement? • How are the "talk early, talk often" children balancing talking and listening? • How do varied groupings or partnerships affect individual and collective participation in talk? • Am I noticing a difference in participation between facilitated talk and independent talk? In what way?
What is the strength of the community around the talk?	• Do children seem to value each other's thoughts? • How are children supporting each other as they construct meaning? • How do varied groupings or partnerships affect this? • Am I noticing a difference in community support between facilitated talk and independent talk? In what way?
What is the strength of the resulting meaning making?	• What depth and breadth of understanding are children constructing? How does this relate to their talk? How does this relate to their cognitive strategy work? • How might their meaning making be broadened or deepened? • As children think and talk independently, are they moving from individual exploration to collaboration thoughtfully? • As children think and talk independently, are they lingering with single texts to strengthen understanding? • As children think and talk independently, are they pursuing ideas across multiple texts?
How much facilitation is needed?	Children's process: • What aspect(s) of talk behavior need facilitating? • What aspect(s) of the meaning making need facilitating? • How much facilitating? For all children, or specific individuals? Teacher process: • Is my facilitation invitational, responsive, agentive, and meaning driven? • Does my facilitation seem to be enough, too much, or not enough? • Are there places where I might have handed off some of the facilitation moves to the children?

Noticings

Afterword

Fear Not!

There are seven days in the week.
Someday isn't one of them.

—Unknown

As you consider the power and potential of purposeful talk, what I hope lingers for you are the voices of the children scattered throughout this text. Dominic, Luis, and Ana, whose energy and insistence that the soldier's actions were "all messed up" drove their efforts to unearth new perspectives. Lawrence, whose captivation with ideas rerouted a brave community deeper into a compelling text. Jaylen, whose confusion found a foothold with classmates who are comfortable with the rhythmic shifts of constructing dialogically. Kylee, who tuned in to a classmate's giggle. Miguel, who drew from his world to shift a conversation about what's in a character's heart. And Brandon, whose move from quiet contemplation to a tentative beginning launched an exploration of human interactions.

These children have fully grasped the value of purposeful talk and are taking charge of their process. I'm hopeful you're now in that beginning space of thinking through the first steps—or contemplating continued steps—for building purposeful talk with your students. Of course, both taking first steps and wading in deeper can seem challenging—even a bit scary. We want to dive right in, but then worry gets the best of us.

Yes, there will be wobbles, and yes, many of those wobbles will be ours. We'll make facilitative missteps. We'll talk too much, and we won't give the children a chance. We'll ask all the questions, forgetting children may have questions of their own. We might not recognize a gem in a child's jumble of words.

Our children may wobble, too. No one will talk. Everyone will talk, and no one will listen. They'll hop and skip over tentative thinking without digging in. They'll focus on right answers, or disagree in ways that are less than productive.

Knowing the talk won't be perfect eventually turns worry into fear, and that fear too often keeps us in the safe lane. This tendency to stay in the safe lane isn't unique to teaching. In *The Art of Possibility: Transforming Professional and Personal Life* (2002), coauthor Benjamin Zander, conductor and music director of the Boston Philharmonic, laments over the pressure placed on musicians to perform with technical perfection. This demand, he postures, keeps competent musicians from taking the expressive risks necessary to become great performers.

Yet Zander wisely points out, "it is only when we make mistakes that we can really begin to notice what needs attention. In fact, I will actively train my students that when they make a mistake, they are to lift their arms in the air, smile, and say, 'How fascinating!'" (2002, 31).

As a case in point, Zander tells of a young pianist, technically competent, yet whose performance remained, in Zander's words, "earthbound." "Earthbound," as Zander explains it, means understanding the piece intellectually, but lacking the ability to convey the emotion (2002, 118).

As he watched, Zander spied the problem. This technically competent pianist was "a two-buttock" player. He was overly correct in his form, starting with his formal, rigid positioning on the piano stool. This emphasis on "being correct" didn't allow the musician to immerse physically or emotionally and flow with the piece—to "catch the wave of the music." Once the musician relaxed and allowed his body to flow with the music, it soared. Zander proclaimed, "a new distinction was born: the one-buttock player" (2002, 119).

What if we took Zander's advice as teachers? What if, rather than fretting about potential calamities, we embraced the messy, delightfully dynamic nature of purposeful talk, and became, if I may extend the metaphor, a "one-buttock teacher"? By this, I'm not flippantly suggesting an unprepared, seat-of-the-pants stance. Rather, I'm advocating for a willing-ness to just let go a bit, and immerse into the tumult of real talk. Letting go can actually be easier than you think, especially when we adopt a "hack mindset."

The hack mindset is a lever for change that originated with the design company IDEO and the Stanford d.school. The idea of the hack mindset was born out of the realization that both fear and a sense of being over-whelmed often keep us from the first steps toward change, no matter how excited or committed we are. We plan, we meet, we trouble shoot, we revise, we form committees, we see roadblocks . . . and before we know it, another school year has come and gone.

Rather than becoming overwhelmed by the complexity of change, the hack mindset invites us to consider a "nimble and iterative approach" by encouraging action through quick, scrappy steps, or hacks (Madsen 2015). Hacks invite us to

★   start small

★   don't overthink it—just try

★   fail forward.

In the world of dialogic process, starting small may mean talking a bit less to notice what your children do with more space for their voices to emerge. It may be identifying a talk focus for your children, and trying just one or two specific facilitation moves to support that focus. Or, it may mean practicing the mindfulness needed to notice strength in bits of talk and begin trying your hand at feedback.

Find your foothold—your first iterative step. Then, find that one book, the one so compelling it will be impossible for your children *not* to talk about—and just try. Let go. Let them talk. Catch the wave of mean-ing making, and ride alongside them. Listen, notice, nudge.

And, when the inevitable wobbles or missteps happen, lift your arms in the air, smile, and exclaim, "How fascinating!" Delight in the very real humans in front of you. Hold on to your iterative goal, the "why" of what you're doing, and take a next step. Gradually, conversation by conversation, purposeful talk will grow.

Works Cited

Alexander, Robin. 2004. "Talking to Learn." *TES Magazine*. January 30. www.tes.com/news/talking-learn-0.

———. 2008. *Towards Dialogic Teaching: Rethinking Classroom Talk.* North Yorkshire, UK: Dialogos.

Barnes, Douglas. 1992. *From Communication to Curriculum.* Portsmouth, NH: Heinemann.

———. 1996. *On Dialogue*, edited by Lee Nichol. New York: Routledge.

———. 2008. "Exploratory Talk for Learning." In *Exploring Talk in School*, edited by Steve Hodgkinson and Neil Mercer. Thousand Oaks, CA: Sage.

———. 2010. "Why Talk Is Important." *English Teaching: Practice and Critique* 9 (2): 7–10. http://education.waikato.ac.nz/research/files /etpc/files/2010v9n2art1.pdf.

Berra, Yogi. 2002. *When You Come to a Fork in the Road, Take It! Inspiration and Wisdom from One of Baseball's Greatest Heroes.* New York: Hachette Books.

Britton, James. 1970. *Language and Learning.* Coral Gables, FL: University of Miami Press.

———. 1983. "Writing and the Story of the World." In *Explorations in the Development of Writing: Theory, Research, and Practice*, edited by Barry M. Kroll and C. Gordon Wells, 3–30. New York: Wiley.

Bryant, Adam. 2015. "Vivek Gupta of Zensar Technologies: Beware of Hiring People Just Like You." *New York Times*. March 7. www.nytimes.com/2015/03/08/business/vivek-gupta-of-zensar -technologies-beware-of-hiring-people-just-like-you.html.

Cazden, Courtney. 2001. *Classroom Discourse: The Language of Teaching and Learning.* Portsmouth, NH: Heinemann.

Clinton, William. 1997. "State of the Union Address." February 4. The U.S. Capitol. Washington, D.C.

Condon, George E., Jr. 2014. "Howard Baker the Eloquent Listener." June 26. https://www.theatlantic.com/politics/archive/2014/06/howard-baker-the-eloquent-listener/442872/.

De la Peña, Matt. 2018. "A Celebration of Stories with Authors and Illustrators." November 16. National Council of Teachers of English Annual Convention, Houston.

Dewey, John. 1933. *How We Think: A Restatement of the Relation of Reflective Thinking to the Educative Process.* Lexington, MA: D. C. Heath and Company.

Finkes, Bradley J. 2014. "A Personal Gift From Prebys to Salk." June 1: A1. Print. *San Diego Union Tribune.*

Gilbert, Ian. 2018. *There Is Another Way: The Second Big Book of Independent Thinking.* Carmarthen, UK: Independent Thinking Press.

Hancock, Herbie. 2015. *Herbie Hancock: Possibilities.* New York: Penguin.

Herold, Cameron. 2012. "A Eulogy for the Private Office." April 26. www.americanexpress.com/us/small-business/openforum/articles/a-eulogy-for-the-private-office/.

Isaacs, William. 1999. *Dialogue: The Art of Thinking Together.* New York: Random House.

Ivey, Gay. 2010. "Texts That Matter." *Educational Leadership* 67 (6): 18–23.

Ivey, Gay, and Peter Johnston. 2010. "Reading Engagement, Achievement, and Moral Development." Paper presented at the annual meeting of the National Reading Conference/Literacy Research Association, Fort Worth, TX: December 1–4.

————. 2017. "Emerging Adolescence in Engaged Reading Communities." *Language Arts* 94 (3): 159–169.

Johnston, Peter. 1997. *Knowing Literacy: Constructive Literacy Assessment.* Portland, ME: Stenhouse.

————. 2003. "Assessment Conversations." *The Reading Teacher* 57 (1): 90–92.

————. 2004. *Choice Words: How Our Language Affects Children's Learning.* Portland, ME: Stenhouse.

———. 2012a. "Guiding the Budding Writer." *Educational Leadership* 70 (1): 64–67.

———. 2012b. *Opening Minds: Using Language to Change Lives*. Portland, ME: Stenhouse.

Johnston, Peter, Gay Ivey, and Amy Faulkner. 2011. "Talking In Class." *The Reading Teacher* 65 (4): 232–237.

Kahane, Adam. 2007. *Solving Tough Problems: An Open Way of Talking, Listening, and Creating New Realities*. San Francisco, CA: Berrett-Koehler Publishers, Inc.

Kelley, David. 2013. *60 Minutes* interview. CBS. WCBS, New York: January 6. Television.

Madsen, Sally. 2015. "The Hack Mindset for School-wide Change." March 3. www.gettingsmart.com/2015/03/hack-mindset-school-wide-change/.

Martin, Demetri. 2012. *This Is a Book*. New York: Grand Central Publishing.

McCoy, Martha L., and Patrick L. Scully. 2002. "Deliberative Dialogue to Expand Civic Engagement: What Kind of Talk Does Democracy Need?" *National Civic Review* 91 (2): 117–135.

Mehan, Hugh. 1979. *Learning Lessons: Social Organization in the Classroom*. Cambridge, MA: Harvard University Press.

Mercer, Neil, and Steve Hodgkinson. 2008. *Exploring Talk in School*. Los Angeles, CA: Sage.

Miranda, Carolina A. 2016. Quoting Annabelle Selldorf, in "Louis Kahn's Salk Institute, the Building that Guesses Tomorrow, Is Aging—Very, Very Gracefully." November 22. *The Los Angeles Times*.

Newkirk, Thomas. 2012. *The Art of Slow Reading*. Portsmouth, NH: Heinemann.

Nichols, Maria. 2006. *Comprehension Through Conversation: The Power of Purposeful Talk in the Reading Workshop*. Portsmouth, NH: Heinemann.

———. 2008. *Talking About Text: Guiding Students to Increase Comprehension Through Purposeful Talk*. Huntington Beach, CA: Shell.

———. 2009. *Expanding Comprehension with Multigenre Text Sets*. New York: Scholastic.

Nystrand, Martin. 1997. *Opening Dialogue*. New York: Teachers College Press.

Opitz, Michael. 2004. *Listen Hear! 25 Effective Listening Comprehension Strategies*. Portsmouth, NH: Heinemann.

Perkins, David. 2014. *Future Wise: Educating Our Children for a Changing World*. Hoboken, NJ: Jossey-Bass.

Peterson, Ralph. 1992. *Life In A Crowded Place: Making A Learning Community*. Portsmouth, NH: Heinemann.

Rosenblatt, Louise. 1968. *Literature as Exploration*, 3rd ed. New York: Noble and Noble.

Salk Institute for Biological Studies. 2018. www.salk.edu/about/history.html.

Senge, Peter. 1990. *The Fifth Discipline: The Art and Practice of the Learning Organization*. New York: Currency-Doubleday.

Simpson, Alyson, and Neil Mercer. 2010. "Editorial: Douglas Barnes Revisited: If Learning Floats on a Sea of Talk, What Kind of Talk? And What Kind of Learning?" *English Teaching* 9 (2): 1.

Sinek, Simon. 2009. *Start With Why*. New York: Penguin.

Vygotsky, Lev. 1978. *Mind In Society: The Development of Higher Psychological Processes*. Cambridge, MA: Harvard University Press.

Wegerif, Rupert. 2010. *Mind Expanding: Teaching for Thinking and Creativity in Primary Education*. New York: McGraw-Hill.

———. 2013. *Dialogic: Education for the Internet Age*. Routledge: New York.

———. 2016. "What is 'Dialogic Space'?" May 2. www.rupertwegerif.name/blog/what-is-dialogic-space.

Wheatley, Margaret J. 2010. *Finding Our Way: Leadership for an Uncertain Time*. San Francisco, CA: Berrett-Koehler Publishers.

———. 2005. *The World Café: Shaping Our Future Through Conversations That Matter*. San Francisco, CA: Berrett-Koehler Publishers.

Wilson, Daniel Gray. 2007. "Team Learning in Action: An Analysis of the Sensemaking Behaviors in Adventure Racing Teams as They Perform in Fatiguing and Uncertain Contexts." Harvard University PhD dissertation.

Zander, Rosamund Stone, and Benjamin Zander. 2002. *The Art of Possibility: Transforming Professional and Personal Life*. New York: Penguin Books.

Zhao, Yong. 2009. "Needed: Global Villagers." *Educational Leadership* 67 (1): 60–65.

Children's Books

Applegate, Katherine. 2014. *Ivan: The Remarkable True Story of the Shopping Mall Gorilla*. New York: Clarion Books.

Arnosky, Jim. 1991. *Raccoons and Ripe Corn*. New York: HarperCollins.

Bunting, Eve. 2003. *Whales Passing*. New York: Scholastic.

———. 2004. *A Picnic in October*. New York: Harcourt, Brace and Company.

Cherry, Lynne. 1990. *The Great Kapok Tree: A Tale of the Amazon Rainforest*. Boston: HMH Books for Young Readers.

Fox, Mem. 1989. *Wilfred Gordon McDonald Partridge*. New York: Kane/Miller.

Grimes, Nikki. 2002. *My Man Blue*. New York: Puffin Books.

Grimm, Edward. 2000. *The Doorman*. New York: Orchard Books.

Hansard, Peter. 2001. *A Field Full of Horses*. Somerville, MA: Candlewick Press.

Hill, Laban Carrick. 2010. *Dave the Potter: Artist, Poet, Slave*. New York: Little, Brown and Company.

Lê, Minh. 2018. *Drawn Together*. New York: Disney-Hyperion.

Lee, Suzy. 2008. *Wave*. San Francisco: Chronicle Books.

Ludwig, Trudy. 2013. *The Invisible Boy*. New York: Knopf.

McCutcheon, John. 2006. *Christmas in the Trenches*. Atlanta: Peachtree.

McMillan, Bruce. 1995. *Nights of the Pufflings*. Boston: Houghton Mifflin Harcourt.

Penn, Audrey. 2006. *A Pocket Full of Kisses*. Terre Haute, IN: Tanglewood Press.

Reynolds, Jason. 2017. *Long Way Down*. New York: Atheneum.

Ruurs, Margriet. 2016. *Stepping Stones: A Refugee Family's Journey*. British Columbia, Canada: Orca Book Publishers.

Rylant, Cynthia. 1996. *An Angel for Solomon Singer*. New York: Scholastic.

Sanna, Francesca. 2016. *The Journey*. London, UK: Flying Eye Books.

Shannon, David. 1998. *No, David!* New York: Scholastic.

Thomas, Angie. 2018. *The Hate U Give*. New York: Balzer + Bray.

Tsuchiya, Yukio. 1997. *The Faithful Elephants: A True Story of Animals, People, and War*. Boston: Houghton Mifflin Harcourt.

Waddell, Martin. 2001. *A Kitten Called Moonlight*. Somerville, MA: Candlewick Press.

Woodson, Jacqueline. 2012. *Each Kindness*. New York: Penguin Books.

Yolen, Jane. 2016. *What To Do With a Box*. Mankato, MN: Creative Editions.

It is better to debate a question without settling it than to settle it without debate.

—Joseph Joubert

What's the difference?	Transferring facilitation
This shifts us from judging and dismissing seemingly disconnected thinking to involving children in decisions about the constructive potential of their thought, or explaining their evolution of thought.	*Are you wondering what led Bobby to this thought? How might you ask him?*
Shifts us from scolding children for lapses in listening to developing their awareness of their own listening, and teaches strategies for remedying lapses in listening.	*How can we get ready to listen?* *What might you do if you realize your listening slipped?*
Shifts us away from telling children to listen. Offers suggestions for developing an active listening stance.	*What are you listening for?*
Shifts us from a parade of new text, new conversation each day to lingering inside books. Teaches the power of one aspect of reflection—allowing someone's words to linger in our minds, "relistening" to them, and realizing greater potential in them.	*Are you wondering if anyone thought more about our ideas last night? How might you ask?*
Shifts us from dismissing confusing thinking to valuing and actively clarifying others' thoughts.	*Did anyone notice the look on Joey's face? Do you think he needs Hallie to say more about her thinking?* *If you're confused, what might you ask to help you understand?*
Shifts us away from a round-robin model of "talk as telling." Teaches specific ways of lingering with a thought and working with it.	*How will you work with Ari's thinking?*
Shifts us from quick checking on agreement and disagreement as a "vote" to digging into agreement and disagreement for the purpose of deepening and broadening thinking.	*Should you explore other reasons why this makes sense?* *What will you do with different thinking?*
Shifts us from pre-scripted questions to questions that genuinely respond to children's thoughts and meaning-making process and nudge for more.	*Why are you wondering about that thought?*
Shifts us away from an assumption that children have connected the bits of conversation into a meaningful whole. Supports a habit of pausing to bundle thinking into that meaningful whole.	*Where are we in our thinking? How do these pieces fit together? What should we hold on to as we read on?*

A full-size version of this table can be downloaded from http://hein.pub/biggerideas (click on Companion Resources).